SQUARE ONE

Where to Start When Following Jesus

ZACH WRIGHT
WITH J. SCOTT DUVALL

Square One: Where to Start When Following Jesus
Copyright © 2020 by Zach Wright and J. Scott Duvall

ISBN: 979-8-6600-9146-9
Independently Published

Scripture quotations marked CSB have been taken from the Christian Standard Bible®, Copyright © 2017 by Holman Bible Publishers. Used by permission. Christian Standard Bible® and CSB® are federally registered trademarks of Holman Bible Publishers.

All rights reserved. For permission requests or to contact the authors, write to square1book@gmail.com.

Front cover image: Zach Wright and Berkley McFarlin.
Book Design: Zach Wright.

To the people of Ennis:
You took my family in and gave us a place to call home.
We love you more than you could ever know.
This book is for you.

Contents

Foreword   **9**

1. Why am I reading this book?   **11**

2. What is God's story?   **21**

3. What does God's story have to do with my story?   **35**

4. Where are you?   **45**

5. I have decided to follow Jesus… Now what?   **55**

6. How do I make my relationship status official?   **63**

7. Is the Holy Spirit a ghost?   **73**

8. Is it possible to have a conversation with God?   **83**

9. The Bible is such a big book… Do I have to read it?   **93**

10. Do I need friends who also follow Jesus?   **105**

11. Where do I go from here?   **115**

Afterword   **127**

A NOTE TO PASTORS AND SPIRITUAL LEADERS

I wrote this book because I need this book. As a pastor, I work with people who want to follow Jesus or are brand new to the idea. I have struggled to find a resource that is easy-to-read without compromising on the truth. So, I decided to write one. This book can be used by individuals that you're working with or by groups of people desiring to learn together. My hope is that it strengthens your churches by developing a strong foundation for new believers. If people don't start well, it will be difficult for them to continue growing in their relationship with God. This book aims to give each person a strong beginning.

-Zach Wright

FOREWORD

A good beginning is essential to almost anything, whether it be starting school or learning how to ride a bike or launching a business or initiating a new relationship. The same is true for beginning the Christian life. So much along the way depends on how we begin. Sadly, there are very few reliable resources to help us begin well. Most resources are either too detailed and academic or too limited and elementary. Zach Wright's *Square One* provides just what people need to begin well as a follower of Jesus.

Zach is a local church pastor in Texas who serves in the trenches of ministry. He has the education and experience to have something valuable to say about how people should begin the Christian life well. I serve as a teacher at a Christian college where I've taught students how to understand and apply the Bible for over thirty years. I've also had the privilege of writing many books. My job with *Square One* has been to edit what Zach has written to add a bit of experience to the mix.

Why am I excited about this book? Because we need this resource in the church. We need rock-solid biblical theology explained in plain language. This book was written for people who are beginning their journey of following Jesus. We have provided the first steps, both in terms of what you need to know and do. Of course, there is more to say on almost every topic we cover, but this is a good place to begin, a trustworthy place.

I've always thought new believers should have a reliable guide for beginning well, and we pray this will be once such resource. Enjoy! And share it with other people in your church and with your church leaders so that they can benefit from a clear and reliable guide for beginning the Christian life well.

-J. Scott Duvall

1

WHY AM I READING THIS BOOK?

Someone is probably making you read this book. If you're married, maybe it's your spouse. Perhaps it's a friend, a family member, or a spiritual leader in your life. You may not even want to read this, and you plan to skim enough of it to make them happy. And you know what? That's ok. It doesn't hurt my feelings. I'm just glad you're reading it.

But I think there is some part of you that knows you might need this. You've wanted to get this "Jesus thing" right for a while, and you can't figure it out. You've looked for it in different ways, but something is missing. Here's my encouragement—you can do this! It's not that complicated. I do want to be careful when I say that because I don't want any confusion. While following Jesus is not complicated, it isn't always easy. There's a difference between complicated and difficult.

Complicated requires a ton of steps that are hard to understand. Difficult means the steps are clear, but they aren't always easy to do. But what if I told you that learning how to follow Jesus could fill the emptiness that you feel inside? What if I told you that you never have to doubt who you are or what you're meant to be? You can skim the rest if you want to, but I think you secretly want to be here.

Every morning at my house starts with a pot of coffee. We are "those people." The "Don't talk to me until I've had my coffee" people. I like to drink my coffee black. It's easier that way. I pour it into the cup, drink it, and let it wake me up. My wife, Ashley, does it differently. She has to put just the right amount of cream in her coffee. Then she reheats it because the cream has cooled it off. She says she can't live without it. Here's the thing, though. When she finishes and takes her cup to the sink, there is usually more than three-quarters of the coffee left! I don't think she likes coffee. I think she likes the idea of coffee. She wants to know that it's there. She loves to smell it. She enjoys letting the cup warm her hands. She likes what it could do for her. But I don't think she likes to drink it. The idea of it wakes her up more than the coffee itself!

Many of us likely treat our relationship with God the same way that Ashley treats coffee. We say that we can't live without him. We tell everyone that we believe in him. We love the idea that he's there. We love the idea of praying to him if life gets hard. Like Ashley and her coffee, we find comfort in the idea of God rather than in a real relationship with him.

Did you know that there is a difference between believing in God and knowing and following Jesus? Many people say they believe in God. Even evil people claim to believe in God. James 2:19 says, "You believe that God is one. Good! Even the demons believe—and they shudder." Even evil spirits accept that God is real! It's not enough for us to just believe there is a God. It's not enough to go to church or to try to be a good person. The only way that we truly experience God in a real relationship is by following Jesus, the Son of God.

It's important to use terms like "following Jesus" or "Christ-follower." Words like "religious," "God-fearing," or even the word "Christian" don't always fully catch what it means to be in a real relationship with Jesus these days. There are so many things described as "Christian" that don't represent Jesus in any way. There are Christian organizations, Christian politicians, Christian nations, and even just regular Christian people who believe in God but don't reflect who Jesus is. The term "Christian" often just means a person who believes there is a God, goes to church sometimes and generally holds to good, moral values. But having a real relationship with Jesus Christ and following him requires a whole different set of priorities!

Many people seem to be content to think that believing in God is enough because there are so many stereotypes of what a Christian is. When I worked at a restaurant right out of college, I got to see some of these stereotypes firsthand. Our restaurant was in a town with a ton of churches. And one of our busiest times of the week was Sunday lunch. Most of our waiters hated working Sunday lunch. Can you guess why? Church people! Now don't hear me wrong. Millions of amazing "church people" exist, and not all of the church people at the restaurant acted that way. However, so many of them fed into the stereotype of religious people who didn't represent Jesus very well. On average, they were the hardest customers to deal with. They were the type of people who would order lemons, sugar, and water. And every waiter was thinking, "Just pay $2 for the lemonade!" They were the kind of people who were very picky about their order and complained a lot. They were also the ones who would leave terrible tips. Or even worse, they would leave no tip at all and a little gospel tract or religious booklet that tells you, the waiter, that you need Jesus. Who wants to follow Jesus after that example?

Just believing that God exists and following Jesus may seem like a subtle distinction, but in reality, there is a vast difference. Just accepting that there is a God might be a comfortable way to live that allows God into our lives when we need him. But it won't let him tell us how to live. We want God around when someone is sick. Or we need him there when we face big problems. Or maybe we want him there in our politics. However, when he confronts us with standing up for what is right when it costs us something or convicts us of a sin that we don't want to give up, it's much easier to keep God at a safe distance. We don't need him asking us to make changes in our lives. Believing that there is a God means that we only use him when it's convenient. We are the Lord or boss of our own lives (at least we think so), and we bring God in when it works to our advantage.

Following Jesus is different. Following Jesus requires real life change. It means letting him take control. It means letting him set the priorities for our lives. Living that way is not an easy thing to do. Whether we want to admit it or not, we like to be in control. That is probably the reason why we don't have self-driving cars yet. We love the idea of them. We understand that they are safer on average than human drivers because they never get distracted. We have been talking about them for a long time, and the technology is there to make them a reality. But they aren't common yet. We are still a pretty long way from self-driving cars becoming the norm.

I think I know the reason why. Picture this for a moment—you walk up to a car, get in the driver's seat, and sit down. You look in front of you, and there is no steering wheel. You look down, and there is no gas pedal. Even scarier, there is no brake pedal. You look all around, and there isn't a single device that gives you control of the car. You're in the driver's seat, but you're still just a passenger. You are entirely at the mercy of the computer that is driving the car. That mental picture freaks us out because we don't have any control over anything. Many of us also feel that same way when we think about letting Jesus take control of our lives. We like the idea of him driving, but only when we allow him. (Or in the words of Carrie Underwood, "Jesus, take the wheeeel..."—sorry couldn't help it.)

But have we ever stopped to think about where we are headed on our own? We don't like giving up control, but we also don't like acknowledging that we're not doing that great of a job on our own. We aren't perfect, and we make many bad choices that hurt ourselves and others. We make choices that we know aren't right and then get frustrated when there are negative consequences. We blame God even though we had control of the steering wheel. But letting Jesus take control is like getting into a self-driving car that will never fail you. It will take you to a destination that you could have never driven to on your own.

Even though following Jesus is difficult, it brings so much joy that we could never find on our own. Many of us are frustrated with following Jesus because we expect our circumstances to change. But that is a problem with our expectations and not with who Jesus is. The Bible never promises to change our circumstances. There is no promise that you will become rich or have perfect health or relationships. Part of this life is dealing with things we cannot control. And that's not a bad thing the more you think about it.

If somehow you were able to snap your fingers and become wealthy or perfectly healthy, would you really be happier? Maybe for a short time, but you would still end up in a place of emptiness because health and wealth can't adequately fulfill your deepest needs.

Everyone, regardless of circumstances, has to face the fact that this life can't offer them everything they need. Because of that, God offers us something so much better than fleeting happiness. He provides a relationship with Jesus that gives meaning, depth, and joy to our lives. Our circumstances don't change when we follow Jesus. We change—and that's even better.

John 6:47 says "Truly I tell you, anyone who believes has eternal life." All throughout Jesus' life, he taught about or was asked about eternal life. When we hear this term "eternal life," it's natural to think of something we will receive one day in Heaven. Did you know that it refers to something that we can have here and now in this life? Eternal life is a future gift, but it is also a present gift. When you follow Jesus, eternal life starts right away. The promises that come with eternal life are available to you now. Because of eternal life, you can learn the difference between joy (a virtue that never changes) and happiness (a fleeting emotion). Eternal life will enable you to face any circumstance with a peace that "surpasses all understanding" (Phil. 4:7). It allows you to face hopeless injustices with strength that only Jesus can provide.

Eternal life gives you hope even when life throws you the worst it has to offer. It means that even though you can't change your circumstances, you can face any of them with the confidence that only comes from Jesus Christ. Can you imagine living a life like this? It doesn't come from only believing there is a God and hoping he shows up when you need him. It doesn't come from making an appearance at church just because we're supposed to. It doesn't come from trying to be like other Christians or trying to do good things. It only comes from following Jesus. It's not complicated. The steps are clear. This life is possible for anyone who learns how to follow Jesus and let him take control.

So how do we do that? It's a beautiful metaphor to say that we want Jesus to take the wheel and take control, but how do we do it in a way that practically affects our lives? If you're looking for more than just religion or a superficial faith, keep reading. This book might be just what you're looking for.

DISCUSSION QUESTIONS

1. Why are you reading this book?

2. What do you think of when you hear the term "Christian?"

3. What is the difference between believing that there is a God and following Jesus?

4. Do you struggle with giving up control?

5. What does "eternal life" mean to you

2

WHAT IS GOD'S STORY?

One of my favorite movies is *The Prestige*. If you've never seen it, I'm about to spoil it. It came out in 2006, though, so I don't really feel bad about giving away the ending. In the movie, two illusionists compete to one-up each other for the ultimate magic trick and the fame and adoration that come with performing it. One of the illusionists, Alfred Borden, manages to create a show where he teleports from one side of the stage to another in just a matter of moments. This trick catapults Alfred into fame and fortune. At the same time, his rival, Robert Angier, obsesses over figuring out how he does it and how he can match it.

The drama builds toward the end of the movie when finally, it is revealed that Alfred has a secret twin brother that no one knows about, not even his own wife. And he seamlessly "teleports" by placing his secret twin in just the right position to finish the show. It's a twist no one sees coming and leaves you shocked as the movie ends. It makes you wonder how two twin brothers could dedicate themselves so profoundly to their craft that they lead secret lives.

I love stories, like this one, that make you think. These stories typically end with a resolution that you never see coming. They make you question something about yourself or human nature. Stories with endings like this are deeply satisfying because they provide us closure in an unexpected way. They solve problems and offer solutions. Did you know that God's story is set up this way? If we heard it for the first time or saw it portrayed in a movie with no prior knowledge, the ending would blow our minds and leave us stunned.

I think we don't appreciate God's story because we've become numb to it. We have heard versions of it over the years, and the power of it has been lost on us. But when we see God's story from beginning to end, we realize that God has had a plan to save us in a way that we could never have predicted. It's a story that offers closure in a deeply satisfying way. It's also a story that provides us answers to life's hardest questions better than any other story could.

We find God's story in the Bible. It's often seen as a big book that seems impossible to read (It's not, but more on that in a later chapter). The Bible contains many small stories that are interwoven into one big story. Because it's such a big book, we struggle to put the parts of the story together. We've heard stories as kids growing up or maybe in sermons at church, but we've never connected the big story from beginning to end. God's story consists of a few significant parts—**Creation** (already happened), **The Fall** (already happened), **Israel's Story** (already happened), **Jesus Christ** (already happened), **The Church's Story** (still happening), and **Final Resolution** (yet to come). When we hear it from start to finish, it really puts into perspective for us how much God loves us and wants to be in a relationship with us. Here is a brief summary of God's Story.

Creation

In the beginning, God's plan was perfect. He created everything that exists, including humans, and for a time, his creation existed in complete harmony. The first humans, Adam and Eve, lived with God in a place called the Garden of Eden. They worked the Garden and spent time with God enjoying the fruits of it. God told Adam and Eve that they could eat from any tree in the Garden except for one—The Tree of the Knowledge of Good and Evil. If they ate from it, God said that they would face the certainty of death. Life in the Garden for Adam and Eve was free of death, decay, and sorrow. Everything was the way it was meant to be. One day, Satan took the form of a snake, came to Adam and Eve, and tempted them to eat from the forbidden tree. He said things like, "You won't actually die. God is keeping this from you because he knows that if you eat it, you will become like him, and he doesn't want that." Adam and Eve believed Satan's lies and ate from the forbidden tree. (Creation can be found in Genesis 1-3.)

The Fall

And just like that, everything changed. Sin came into the world. And with it came decay, sorrow, and death. From that point on, every human that ever lived would have to face the difficulties of life. (Plus, every human who has ever lived also believed the lies of Satan and disobeyed God.) But God didn't give up on us. Even though humans destroyed their relationship with God through sin, he still devised a way to set us free. Eventually, God will restore us to the way of life that Adam and Eve experienced in the Garden of Eden. He set in motion a plan that would make things right so that we could eventually return to a perfect relationship with our Creator.

Because actions have consequences, Adam and Eve were banished from the Garden and, as a result, banished from directly being in the presence of God. This was very painful for everyone involved. However, God's presence was still available to everyone in an indirect way. He continued to stay involved with his creation as Adam and Eve had children and their descendants populated the earth. This new world that they lived in was much different from the Garden. Because of Adam and Eve's sin, people had knowledge of evil and began to make evil choices. People got so out of control that God had to send a great flood to destroy all of the earth except for one righteous man and his family—Noah. (The Fall can be found in Genesis 4-9.)

Israel's Story

Even after Noah, things didn't get much better. Men and women trusted in their own ways instead of God's way and continued to make evil choices. Finally, God began the next step in his plan by bringing himself one step closer into a restored relationship with his people. Through a man named Abraham, God established a promise that would allow his descendants to become God's people. It wasn't the final solution, but it was a step in the right direction. A few generations after Abraham, a man named Moses wrote down God's laws for his people. He established these laws as a way of life for those who wanted to be restored to God's original plan. God was slowly making things right with his people.

For many generations, God's people lived under these laws. God's laws were good. When followed perfectly with the right intentions, they led his people into a right relationship with him. However, when someone disobeyed God's Laws or cared more about following the rules than living out the purpose behind the law, there were negative consequences. These laws were for the benefit of God's people, but sadly, no one was capable of living up to God's good standard. Because the Israelites failed to live God's way, God couldn't use them to do the bigger job of restoring his whole creation. A pattern emerged with God's people that continued for hundreds of years.

```
        The Israelites doubted and rejected God.
              ↗                    ↘
The Israelites         ←         An enemy
repented and                     persecuted and
returned to God.                 conquered Israel.
```

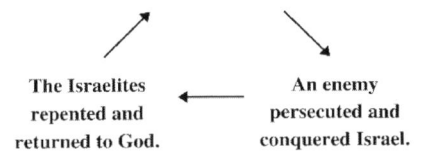

The Israelites tried their best to follow God's way, but they continually came up short. They continually doubted and rejected God even when he remained faithful to them. They followed this cycle for hundreds of years, but because of God's great love, he never gave up on them. A common theme began to arise for those that were considered to be righteous during this time. Those who were in right relationship with God were living the way God had designed humans to live. They were working toward his broader mission of restoring creation. Those who weren't in right relationship disobeyed his laws completely.

Or they obsessed over them so much that they forgot that their purpose was to bring them into a relationship with God. Even when there were laws, righteousness wasn't really about following the rules. It was about seeking a relationship with God. The final chapter of the Israelite's cycle of disobedience ended with God's people being taken from their land and into exile by a conquering nation. God's people were now without a home, without hope, and in desperate need of help. And God's plan was definitely in jeopardy. (Israel's Story can be found starting in Genesis 10 and continuing through the rest of The Old Testament.)

Jesus Christ

But God wasn't finished with them. As a matter of fact, he had the best thing waiting for them. God sent his Son Jesus into the world to finish what he started. And not only was Jesus coming to restore God's people, but he was coming to restore everything. The Christmas Story tells us how Jesus was born, and the Easter Story tells us how Jesus died and rose from the dead. (If you only went to church on Christmas and Easter because your mom or grandma made you, you've probably heard these stories before.) Jesus came to preach a different way. He began to show people how God wanted us to live. Because no one until that point had gotten it right, Jesus came to fulfill the plan that God had to bring his people back into a relationship with himself. His teachings were so radical that it divided people into two groups. Some ran toward him and accepted God's way. And some ran away from him and hated the message that he brought.

Jesus lived a perfect life. Seriously, he did. The Bible tells us that he never committed a single sin, and somehow he navigated the difficulties of life without ever messing up. It's significant that we believe that because if we don't, his death doesn't mean anything for us. Jesus was persecuted for what he was teaching. Eventually, he was put to death on the cross. Maybe you've heard this part of the story before? After he died, they put him in a tomb, but on the third day, he rose from the dead. After his resurrection from the dead, he continued spending time with his followers for 40 days. On his last day, he ascended into Heaven, promising to one day return and bring final restoration to God's people. And ever since that day, having a relationship with God has been all about following Jesus. (Jesus' Story can be found in The Gospels—Matthew, Mark, Luke and John.)

The Church's Story

In addition to final resolution in the future, Jesus also promised to send the Holy Spirit to his followers as a way of living in God's presence while he was gone. Following his ascension into Heaven, Jesus' followers finally understood what he did through his death and resurrection. They began to spread the good news to everyone they knew. They began to meet together in groups, thanking God and encouraging one another. After a few days, the Holy Spirit came in a powerful event called Pentecost and filled each one of Jesus' followers with God's presence.

Since Pentecost, every person who chooses to repent and follow Jesus becomes a part of the Church and receives the gift of the Holy Spirit (more on this gift in Chapter 7). Think about that for a minute. If you are a follower of Jesus, you are living out the same mission that millions of others have for the last 2,000 years. It gives me encouragement to know that. I am not the only one that has had to struggle through this life, trying to figure everything out. There are so many others who have gone before, faithfully showing us what it means to follow Jesus. As God's Church, we live out his kingdom here and now while waiting for Jesus to return. We are not alone. We are part of a larger community throughout history and across the world that is building God's Kingdom in this life, waiting for God's plan to fully be complete. (The early church's story can be found in Acts-Jude.)

Final Resolution

The final work of Jesus is still yet to come. He promised us that he would someday return to destroy evil once and for all and restore God's creation back to the way it was in the beginning. This promise gives us hope—and not the kind of hope where we wait, wishing for something to happen. He provides us with the kind of hope where we wait, knowing that something is going to happen. It is a sure hope, and there is no need for us to doubt it. This hope is what sets us apart. It is what allows us to navigate pain and suffering in this life. We grieve and mourn the hard times, but we do so, knowing that this is not how things are supposed to be. We look forward to the day when Jesus returns, and everything will be made right again. (The promises of Final Resolution can be found in Revelation.)

"Look, God's dwelling is with humanity, and he will live with them. They will be his peoples, and God himself will be with them and will be their God. He will wipe away every tear from their eyes. Death will be no more; grief, crying, and pain will be no more, because the previous things have passed away." (Revelation 21:3-4)

Whew, that was a lot. Did you keep track of it all? It's ok if you didn't. That was a few thousand years in just a few paragraphs. Here's what it all means—*God created us because he wants a relationship with us.* Have you ever stopped to think about that? God didn't have to create us, but he chose to do it anyway. The way that things were with Adam and Eve in the Garden of Eden is what God desires for us—a perfect relationship with him in a perfect world. And even when we messed up his plan, he stayed with us. He didn't let us go. No matter how many times we failed him with our bad choices, he remained faithful to us.

Because God is righteous and holy, when we decided to bring sin into the world, our actions required a consequence. No choices in life can exist without consequences, and there were many consequences to our sin. Sin brought death into the world. Sin brought brokenness that causes pain in this life. And most importantly, sin ruined our relationship with God. A holy God couldn't compromise with unholiness. Something had to make right the wrong that we have done. And that's where Jesus comes into the story. Not just anyone could make our sin right. It had to be someone that didn't deserve it but chose to do it anyway. So Jesus, God's Son, came to fix all the consequences that our sin caused.

This is where our story becomes a part of God's story. We are all living a story whether we realize it or not. And every single one of us is looking for ways to give our story meaning and purpose. We look for validation from others. We work to achieve status, or we let our culture drive who we are. We find our meaning in our work, our hobbies, or loved ones around us. And while not all of those are bad things, none of them can really give our story a satisfying purpose. Eventually, all of them come up short. Only God's story can provide what we need to meet our deepest needs of purpose and meaning.

Maybe you've heard the verse, John 3:16, before. It gets thrown around a lot. Athletes put it on their equipment. Politicians quote it as their favorite Bible verse. Christians put it on billboards. It gets used for a good reason. But it seems like the overuse of it has robbed the verse of its power. Look at what it says—"For God loved the world in this way: He gave his one and only Son, so that everyone who believes in him will not perish but have eternal life." Let that really sink in for a minute. This verse is so popular because it's probably the most concise description of God's story. On our own, we deserve death because every single one of us has sinned. But God loved us so much that he sent Jesus to suffer and die in our place so that we don't have to. Based on our actions, we deserve what Jesus went through. But through the most gracious and loving act in history, he took our punishment and gave us life. He gave us the promise that our relationship with God will be restored to its original design.

Talk about an unexpected ending that provides closure in a profoundly satisfying way! The Good Father gave his only Son to save the people who didn't deserve it. If you heard this story for the first time, you never would have seen the ending coming. You would never have guessed that God's love for us would be so great that he would sacrifice himself to restore a relationship that we destroyed. The best part is, this isn't just a story or a movie. After reading stories or watching movies, we finish them and then go on with our lives. But this story is different. This story becomes a part of our life.

Only God's story can show us why we're on earth and what we're supposed to do while we're here. Isn't that what we're all looking for? The answers to the meaning of life? We live on a planet with 7.8 billion other people in the only known environment that can sustain human life. We are born, we live, and then we die. What does it all mean? Many religions and scientists have tried to answer this question, but all rely on human effort.

I don't know about you, but I've tried hard to generate meaning on my own, and I always come up short. No matter how hard I work, my own answers can never give me peace. The beauty of God's story is that we don't have to work for meaning. When Jesus died in our place and then rose from the dead, he gave us life when we deserved death because of our sin. Because of his death and resurrection, he gives us value, worth, and meaning based on who *he is* and not who we are. Our story becomes a part of his story. It doesn't matter who we have been or what we have done. He gives us the chance to make his story our own and to find meaning in the most deeply satisfying way. I don't know about you, but that's the story I want to live.

DISCUSSION QUESTIONS

1. What is God's story?

2. Which part of God's story was new to you?

3. Why do you believe God created us?

4. How does God's story give you hope?

5. How have you tried to give your story meaning on your own? How did that turn out?

3

WHAT DOES GOD'S STORY HAVE TO DO WITH MY STORY?

I have an older brother that I love and respect so much. His name is Erik, and he's a great person. But as a younger brother, I would never say that to his face (just in print for everyone to read). Picking at an older brother is a natural instinct that is ingrained into almost every younger brother. As the younger brother, I was always smaller and weaker than my older brother growing up. I could never beat him in a fair fight. So I had to resort to other ways. Because I couldn't beat him physically, I had to look for psychological advantages. My main tactic usually consisted of finding a way to blame him for something I had done or started. It usually went something like this—I would provoke him or punch him when he wasn't looking. He would hit me back, and then I would yell, "Mom! Dad! Erik's hitting me!" Then, they would say "Erik! Leave your little brother alone! Be nice to him." I'm not proud of this (well, maybe a little). I loved finding ways to blame him and resorting to the "Erik made me do it" argument. Now that we're adults, things have definitely changed, and we're much wiser and more... Ok fine. It's still something I'm working on. Old habits die hard.

Putting the blame on others is something that comes naturally to us. It's much easier when we don't have to face the consequences of our actions. One of the most refreshing things you can find is someone who owns up to their mistakes. Any time a public figure messes up, you often see them deny or minimize their offense (think of people like Lance Armstrong, Roger Clemmons, or Bill Clinton). Eventually, they might admit to it, but after so many lies, it's tough to feel sorry for them. But when someone stands up and says, "I made a mistake. It was my choice, and I'm sorry. I promise to get better and try to make it right," it's like a breath of fresh air. Think of the examples in your own life. When someone has hurt you, and they own up to it and apologize, it means so much. Also, think about how hard it is to do the same when you have hurt someone else. It's not an easy thing to do, but it makes everything better.

If we wanted to, we could blame Adam and Eve for the world we live in. We just worked through God's story, and all the bad stuff started when they made a choice to disobey God. We could say, "I was born a sinner because of their choices" or, "It's not my fault that I do bad things. The world is a bad place." But if we do that, we're taking the route of denying or minimizing our own offenses. If we're really honest with ourselves, we are responsible for the choices we've made. No one has forced us to do anything, and even when we have felt helpless, we always had an opportunity to do the right thing. Every single one of us has messed up and disobeyed God, just like Adam and Eve. Anyone who tells you differently is lying (and adding to the list).

This is not a popular thing to say, but those choices are called "sin." It's a harsh way to describe it, but it's necessary. More than just messing up or making mistakes, we have sinned against God. Even the best person we can think of in history, besides Jesus himself, has sinned. We could try to make excuses by saying that our own life circumstances were so bad that we couldn't help it. But can we say that we had it worse than Jesus did? He faced persecution and unimaginable suffering and still managed to live God's will through it all. This isn't a knock on us or an attempt to minimize some of the terrible life circumstances that we've faced. It merely shows that we've tried our best to get it right, but all of us have failed. Romans 3:23 says, "For all have sinned and fall short of the glory of God." This verse doesn't leave room for us to place blame on anyone else. Every single one of us falls short on our own.

Now for some good news—while falling short may be our fault, we have been given the gift of breaking free from our sin. Because of Jesus, our relationship with God can be restored. The consequences of our sin were death and separation from God, but Jesus came to suffer the consequences for us. By dying on the cross and then rising from the dead three days later, Jesus defeated sin and death and made a way for us to be put back into a relationship with God. There is no greater gift than that!

Have you ever been given a gift you didn't deserve? It's hard for many of us to accept gifts like that. We have this need to earn things. That may be one of the reasons why it is so hard for many of us to accept this gift of freedom and restoration that Jesus gave to us. We don't deserve it. We didn't do anything to earn it. As a matter of fact, we have a mountain of mistakes in our past that tell us we deserve the opposite of what Jesus offers us. It may seem trivial, but all we have to do to receive this free gift is to acknowledge that we are not good enough on our own and accept the life that Jesus offers to us.

Only when we acknowledge that can we allow our story to become a part of God's story. It's better this way. If becoming a part of God's story required us to earn it, it wouldn't mean as much. It would be all about how much we're capable of doing. *God's plan for us was always about what he did and not what we could do.* Economic status, social status, and anything else we've earned carry no weight in God's Kingdom. This puts all of us on a level playing field. Only God is good enough, and none of us can earn his love.

The only way that we can be in a relationship with him is through his Son, Jesus Christ. As we saw in the last chapter, Jesus lived a perfect life and then died so that he could take the punishment that we deserved for our sins. Because of what he did, our relationship with

God can be restored. We must assess ourselves honestly and believe it. Once we do that, we become a part of his story and start living it out. This is where we start following Jesus.

So how do we do that? How do we start following Jesus? Or how do we know for sure that we already have a relationship with him? Have you seen the home improvement shows that take an old house and remodel it completely? We tend to think that following Jesus would be like that—a remodel of our lives. But I think we need to be careful with that mindset. We believe that all Jesus needs to do is come into our lives and fix a few things.

But that's not what needs to happen. If we were to compare this to remaking an old house, following Jesus would be more like demolishing the house and starting over completely. He did not come to make our old self better. He came to kill it entirely and to give us a new self. It's not a remodel. It's a total rebuild. Ephesians 4:20-24 says, "But that is not how you came to know Christ, assuming you heard about him and were taught by him, as the truth is in Jesus, to take off your former way of life, the old self that is corrupted by deceitful desires, to be renewed in the spirit of your minds, and to put on the new self, the one created according to God's likeness in righteousness and purity of the truth."

To follow Jesus, we must be prepared to submit to this rebuild. We must make a decision to follow him and be willing to allow him to start the process of transforming our lives.

Like any significant event in our lives, following Jesus involves a "Before," "During" and "After." I think these markers are helpful for us in identifying how to start following Jesus or in affirming that we already have.

"The Before" describes our lives before Jesus came into them. For some people, this might mean a life full of hard living with destructive choices. "The Before" is full of regret and heartache over mistakes that were made. For others, it may mean a very normal life that, on the surface, seems to be mostly good. Maybe there were some minor mistakes here and there, but overall, "The Before" was a good life. This is where we see that Jesus is the great equalizer.

Our "Before" doesn't matter at all. Whether we were considered "bad people" or "good people" by the world's standards is not relevant in God's kingdom. As I said before, none of us, not even the best person among us, has a "Before" that is good enough to meet God's standard. Thankfully, the opposite is also true. The worst person among us does not have a "Before" that cannot be redeemed by God's love. No matter what our "Before" is like, it leads us to "The During."

"The During" describes how we come to know Jesus. Like "The Before," this can be different for everyone. Jesus is the same for all of us, but the way we find him often varies. For those who grew up in denominations like Baptist or Pentecostal, "The During" is often a specific moment they can look back on. They might recall a time when they walked down the aisle or prayed a prayer with someone during a church service. For those who grew up in denominations like Methodist or Catholic, it might be more difficult to recall an exact moment when their relationship with Jesus began. Instead, they might think of a process or a season of life where they could identify that their relationship with Jesus began during that time. For others, it might be some combination of these two. No matter the experience, the most important part is recognizing that a relationship with Jesus started in our lives. This is our "During."

While "The Before" and "The During" may be different for everyone, "The After" is the same. We all leave our old lives behind, whether good or bad, and commit our lives to Jesus. Once we have started that, our lives should be different than before. By following Jesus, our old self is put to death, and a new person is created within us. This new self makes our priority to live the way that Jesus lived; to become more like him. We will not be a perfect person, but we will be a different person. "The After" is a process that never ends. We will never reach a point where we have it all figured out. As long as we are alive on earth, we will continue to grow in our faith.

The key for "The During" and "The After" is to "repent and follow." "Repent" is a word that Jesus often uses to describe recognizing our sin and admitting that we have made mistakes. "From then on Jesus began to preach, 'Repent, because the kingdom of heaven has come near.' As he was walking along the Sea of Galilee, he saw two brothers, Simon (who is called Peter), and his brother Andrew. They were casting a net into the sea—for they were fishermen. 'Follow me,' he told them, 'and I will make you fish for people.' Immediately they left their nets and followed him." (Matthew. 4:17-20)

To receive affirmation that we have a relationship with Jesus, we must be able to look back on our lives and see a time where we changed course. We must be able to see a time where we decided to stop living our own way and invited Jesus in to create a new self that lives his way. We must be like the disciples in these verses. They repented of their sin and then stopped what they were doing to follow Jesus. Before, their world revolved around themselves. After they decided to repent and follow, their world revolved around Jesus. If you have done the same, you are a follower of Jesus.

This is how our story becomes a part of God's story. Once we decide to turn from our sin and follow Jesus, we begin living out God's story in the way that he meant for us to do. We become a part of his plan to restore his kingdom here on earth. Our story receives meaning and purpose when it becomes a part of the greater story that God has been telling since creation. Now that you have heard God's story and understand how it applies to your story, it brings up the most critical question you will ever be asked (and the title of the next chapter)—Where are you?

DISCUSSION QUESTIONS

1. What does God's story have to do with your story?

2. Why is it so easy to blame others for our actions?

3. Why is it hard to accept unearned gifts?

4. What does a "rebuild" instead of a "remodel" mean to you?

5. What does it mean to "repent and follow?"

4

WHERE ARE YOU?

Self-reflection is not something that comes naturally to most of us. When someone asks us how we're doing, we are so busy that we often don't know how to answer that question. Most of the time, we give the "Pretty good, how about you?" answer. It's natural for all of us to glaze over that question in conversation. This is especially tough for guys. The stereotype says that we, as men, don't have feelings. But that's not true. We definitely have feelings. But guys, if you're like me, I have a hard time identifying what they are. It's a huge revelation to acknowledge to my wife, "I feel... sad." It takes effort to identify and voice an emotion, but it is so healthy when I do. Even though it's not good for me, it's easier to ignore my emotions and pretend like they're not there. But this isn't a book about men's feelings. (Thank goodness. I don't want any part of that.)

I think we ignore self-reflection because we're scared of what we might find. We might have to confront some issues or complex things in our lives that we would rather just ignore. Spiritually, we must put in the effort to assess where we have been, where we are, and where we are going. This is the question we ended with in Chapter 3—"Where are you?" We cannot glaze over this question like we do so many other issues in our lives. It is not enough to say, "Yes, I believe in God" or "Yes, I go to church." We must confront questions like "Is Jesus the priority in my life?" or "How has my life changed since Jesus became part of it?" The answers to these questions lead us to growth and healthy places and the kind of life God planned for us.

We read about three parts of following Jesus in the previous chapter—"The Before," "The During," and "The After." All of us fall into one of these three categories, and each one has a next step. I hope that by the end of this chapter, you will clearly identify where you are and see your next step forward. I also want to give a word of caution. Don't overthink this too much. Try to be unbiased in evaluating where you are. My goal is not to manipulate you in any way. I really do believe in honestly assessing ourselves (for better or worse) and using that information to allow God to help us grow. So let the Spirit lead you and be ok with your answer. We all have a lot of growing to do.

The Before

Have you started a relationship with Jesus? If the honest answer to this question is "No," then you fall into this category. If you are unsure of how to answer this question, here are some guidelines that might help you find it. Was there a moment in your life that you made a decision to follow Jesus? Maybe it was at a church service or with a family member when you made a specific decision to give your life to Jesus. Since that time, has your life been different? If there wasn't a particular moment, maybe there was a time when you began taking steps toward Jesus. Either on your own or with someone guiding you, you began to take slow steps toward Jesus. It might have taken place at a young age or when you got older. At the end of the process, were you able to look back and say with confidence that you started a relationship with Jesus? If any of your life experiences lead you to honestly answer "Yes" to this question, then you are not in this category. The next two sections are for you.

There is a middle road here between "Yes" and "No." I know because I've experienced it myself. I made a decision to follow Jesus at a very young age. And throughout my life, I've had times where I doubted how genuine that early decision was. "Did I really mean it?" "Was I old enough to understand?" Perhaps some of you can relate to this. At some point in your life, you made a commitment to follow Jesus. But at a later time, you questioned whether it was an authentic decision. Maybe you made some bad choices and felt like you drifted away from God. Perhaps you experienced times of doubt and deserted God altogether.

My advice for those who find themselves in this middle road is to let God lead you to the right answer. Some need reassurance that a long-ago decision or way of life was real and valid. Others need the conviction to say that it was something you didn't really understand or want to do. There are really two answers here—either God will give you peace and assurance that your decision was real, and no amount of sin or doubt can take that way. Or he will convict you and lead you to make a genuine decision now to follow him for the first time. Whatever answer he leads you to, follow it honestly and take whatever step is next.

If you know for sure that the answer is "No," I applaud you for your honesty. I also encourage you to read on to the next section about how to start a relationship with Jesus. If you feel something inside of you telling you that something is missing in your life, that "something" is most likely the Holy Spirit pulling you toward Jesus. You've tried living your own way, and you have come up short. You have been looking for the answers to life's hardest questions without finding true meaning and purpose. There is an emptiness that nothing seems to fill.

A relationship with Jesus fulfills all of those things. It does not make your life perfect, and it does not make your problems go away. But what it does is change you. It changes your perspective on life, and it shows you what is most important. It causes you to stop living for yourself and instead, to start living as part of God's story. It's ok that your answer to this question is "No." But I strongly encourage you to find a way to change your answer. You can use this opportunity to move from "The Before" to "The During." You can change the answer to this question from "No" to "Yes." It will be the most important decision you ever make.

The During

If you answered "No" to the previous question, do you feel something inside of you pulling you toward Jesus? Are you tired of the way that you have been living, and are you ready to join God's story? If so, then you are in "The During." This is the process of starting a relationship with Jesus and making changes in your life. So how do we do it? How do we start a relationship with Jesus? I think these verses answer that question in a pretty clear way. "If you confess with your mouth, 'Jesus is Lord,' and believe in your heart that God raised him from the dead, you will be saved. One believes with the heart, resulting in righteousness, and one confesses with the mouth, resulting in salvation." (Romans 10:9-10)

If you believe in God's story that was laid out in Chapter 2 where we learn that Jesus died and rose again to take the punishment for your sins, then you are ready to start a relationship with Jesus. I encourage you to stop right now and spend time in prayer, committing this decision to the Lord. Tell him that you are ready to leave your old life. Tell him that you believe in him and what he has done for you. Tell him that you are ready to live as a member of his kingdom. I also encourage you to seek someone out in your life to help you with this decision. Is there a pastor or leader at your church that you trust? If you're not involved with a church, is there a friend or family member who is a Christ-follower that can help guide you through this decision? I feel so strongly about how important this is that I'm willing to talk to you myself. If you have no one in your life that can guide you through this decision, please email me personally (square1book@gmail.com), and I will walk you through it.

Make this decision with courage and conviction and then commit your life to it. It may take some time for this decision to fully take hold in your life, and that's ok. It may involve some changes, but they are changes worth making, even if they take a while. Following Jesus means allowing him to be the priority. It consists of ordering our lives around the ways of his kingdom. If we were living for ourselves before, this might require some hard changes. It doesn't mean that we have to get rid of everything in our lives. It just means that everything that is a part of our lives gets evaluated by a different set of principles.

It may mean changing some habits or friendships. It may mean acknowledging some sin and seeking help to eliminate it. But the good news is, these changes will bring incredible joy and peace. Jesus promises us that he will carry our burdens for us (Matthew 11:30). This doesn't mean that our troubles or problems go away, but it does mean they get lighter because Jesus carries them.

While these changes may be hard, they also bring more benefits and blessings than we could ever imagine. After we make this decision, it leads us to "The After."

The After

Once you arrive here, your answer to the original question, "Have you started a relationship with Jesus" is a resounding "Yes!" There is no need to doubt or question it. If you have started a relationship with Jesus, you are a Christ-follower committed to living his way. It's important to note that after this happens, you will not be a perfect person. Because none of us are perfect, we will still sin and make mistakes even after starting a relationship with Jesus. The main difference here is that as Christ-followers, we are convicted of our sin and do not stay in it. We admit it and ask forgiveness when we mess up. We accept God's mercy and keep moving forward. This is not an excuse to sin or do whatever we want. Instead, this shows that we are human, and when we mess up, God is big enough to still be present in our lives. Even if you have made mistakes since following Jesus, don't question your relationship with him. Instead, focus on working through your mistakes and keep moving forward. Begin again right where you are! Don't let the shame of your mistakes hinder you from being a part of his kingdom here on earth.

The best part about "The After" is that it never stops. You will never reach a point where you have it all figured out or know all of the answers. Following Jesus isn't really about getting all the answers or achieving a certain level of righteousness. It's about entering a new relationship with the Lord and developing the regular habits that allow us to walk through this life with Jesus guiding the way. We will learn and grow as we progress, but the journey becomes just as important as the destination. Through different seasons of our lives, Jesus will guide us in and out of times of difficulty and times of blessings. There will be both good and bad. There will be life circumstances that we cannot control. But the best part is, we will be moving forward with Jesus at our side. He will show us step by step how to become more like him. "Let us run with endurance the race that lies before us, keeping our eyes on Jesus, the source and perfecter of our faith." (Romans 12:1-2)

When you arrive in this stage, "The After," *live free in the knowledge of your salvation.* You are a child of God who is living out his story. You are not perfect, but in humility, you have accepted the grace that God offers to you. You recognize that this life is not about you. It's about God's great plan being accomplished here on earth. You are doing your part to bring about the resolution to this plan. You are living out the greatest story ever told. You have hope for Christ's future return. Even though this world is full of pain and heartache, you have confidence that it will be resolved one day. You know that God will restore creation back to the way that it was in the beginning. You know that one day you will live in a perfect relationship with your Creator. But until that day, you know how to live now. You know how to live like Jesus.

DISCUSSION QUESTIONS

1. Do you struggle with self-reflection? If so, why?

2. Where are you?

3. Describe your "Before."

4. If you have experienced it, describe your "During."

5. If you have experienced it, describe your "After."

5

I HAVE DECIDED TO FOLLOW JESUS... NOW WHAT?

How many times have you seen an advertisement for a diet or workout program? It has to be in the hundreds or more, right? We see it on TV commercials. We see it on social media. We see it at the gym. We see it everywhere. These ads almost always have a picture of someone looking very fit and promising that you, too, can look just like them if you follow their plan. There is often a before and after picture to show you the incredible transformation that can happen with that plan (and fine print that says "results not typical"). You can have the perfect body and perfect health if you follow a specific diet or workout program. But most people who follow these programs don't see the results they want or they see results for a little while and then go back to the way they used to live.

The problem is that we focus more on the results rather than the lifestyle it takes to achieve lasting results. It's not really rocket science. All of us know what it takes to get into shape. No matter what program you follow, these results come from basically two things—eating healthy and exercising regularly. Easy enough, right? Except junk food is delicious, and crashing on the couch is way more enjoyable than working out. But we don't focus on that part. We focus on the washboard abs that the program promises us. Instead of focusing on changing our lifestyle, we try to follow that particular plan for long enough to get the results of the fit person advertising it. And when we come up short, we go back to the way we were living and blame it on something else. To live healthy lives, we have to commit to a healthy way of life, not a program.

The same is true for following Jesus. We may see people who have a stable relationship with Jesus and want what they have. Maybe they have a strong faith and lead others around them, or they lead their family well. Perhaps they are always helping others and doing the right thing. Maybe they still maintain joy even in the worst circumstances. We look at people like that and want the results that they have. But like the diet and workout programs, we set ourselves up to fail if we focus only on the results and not on the process.

Following Jesus is not about working hard to achieve results. Following Jesus is about committing to a way of life that makes him the priority. This is why Christianity was referred to as "The Way" by the first followers of Jesus (Acts 9:2, Acts 19:9). After we follow "The Way" for a time, results begin to happen. But they only happen because we have committed to the process, not because we have worked hard on our own to achieve them. This idea is often found in the Bible. It's usually referred to as faith and works (I like the term "action"). Faith is the mindset we develop each day to trust in Jesus. Action is the result of that faith. Both are necessary to follow Jesus, but it's essential to distinguish one from the other. If one happens without the other, it leads us off course.

Faith in Jesus is where we start. We trust who he is and decide to live his way. As we do that, action begins to happen in our life because of our faith. If there is no action in our lives, it is hard to say that genuine faith exists. But it's important not to make action the main focus; otherwise, it becomes action without faith and a performance-based faith. Confusing enough? It's kind of like a "chicken and the egg" scenario except, in this case, it does matter which comes first. Faith must come first, but if it's real, genuine faith, action will eventually be there.

But the fruit of the Spirit is love, joy, peace, patience, kindness, goodness, faithfulness, gentleness, and self-control. The law is not against such things (Galatians 5:22-23).

These verses describe the fruit of the Spirit. When we first read them, it seems like we should focus on developing those fruits in our lives. We should try to become more patient and kind. We should try to be more joyful and faithful. But that mindset focuses on the results and not the process. If we read carefully, we realize that all these behaviors are the *fruit* of the Spirit. That means that they are the result of the Spirit working in our lives. Instead of trying to become more patient or kind or joyful or faithful, we should instead focus on allowing the Spirit to work in our lives. We should focus on growing our faith in God so that the Spirit will continue to transform us. As we do that, without even realizing it sometimes, we will start to see the fruit of the Spirit develop. Because of our faith and the Spirit's work, we will have love, joy, peace, patience, kindness, goodness, faithfulness, gentleness, and self-control. These attitudes and actions show that our faith is growing and that the Spirit is at work.

What good is it, my brothers and sisters, if someone claims to have faith but does not have works? Can such faith save him?... Senseless person! Are you willing to learn that faith without works is useless? (James 2:4,20).

We do not focus on actions (works), but they must be present. If they are not, their absence makes our faith "useless." That is a harsh word, but it drives home the point of how our faith must lead to action. If we believe in Jesus, but it does not change anything about how we live, has it really taken hold in our lives? *Genuine faith leads to genuine action.* When neither is done out of pride or selfish ambition, true growth is happening in a follower of Christ. Our faith leads us closer to Jesus. The closer we are to Jesus, the more we have action present in our lives. This action validates the presence of our faith.

"I am the vine; you are the branches. The one who remains in me and I in him produces much fruit, because you can do nothing without me." (John 15:5)

These are Jesus' words describing how we should follow him. The goal is not to produce fruit. The goal is to "remain." Jesus uses this metaphor to describe what our relationship with him should be like. Just like a branch cannot live without the vine, we cannot live without Jesus. A branch depends upon the vine for life-giving nutrients to stay alive. A branch is also able to produce fruit because of the support it receives from the vine. A branch must remain connected to the vine to produce fruit. In the same way, we depend upon Jesus for life-giving growth. And we can produce fruit because of the support we receive from Jesus. We must stay connected to him to produce fruit. When we "remain," we produce fruit. So instead of focusing on producing fruit, we focus on "remaining in Jesus" (more on how we do this in the following chapters). As we do that, there will be fruit (action) in our lives.

We receive salvation from God only because of the grace he gives us through Jesus. We cannot work to earn it. We cannot do enough good things to be worthy of it. However, the result of our salvation should lead us to do good things. For that reason, when a person makes a decision to follow Jesus, there should be some action as a result of that decision. These actions are not earning the grace that has been given. These actions happen because our lives gain new priorities. We are in a new relationship, and our love for Jesus (in response to his love for us) leads us to do good things. We don't do good things so that Jesus will love us. I've said it a lot of different ways, so let me summarize it in an easy way. Here are the two steps that must be done in order:

1. Follow Jesus (Faith) ⟶ **2. Do Good Things (Action)**

In the following chapters, I'm going to explore the most important things that should happen in someone's life after they start following Jesus. I put this chapter before those chapters for a reason. My hope is that you will never lose sight of why we do the things we do to follow Jesus. It's not a checklist of things that we have to do to be a "good Christian." God doesn't want a checklist faith from us. We're not trying to earn God's love. He loved us first. He wants a genuine relationship with us. As we develop that real relationship, we start to do good things.

The best part is, we do them because we want to do them, not because we have to do them. These good works become more natural for us, and they bring us joy as we do them. People who have started to live a healthy and fit lifestyle (like those I mentioned at the beginning of this chapter) develop habits that become second nature. Over time, they learn to focus on the process and not the results. As that happens, they become less concerned about the results even though they are happening. Instead, they become more focused on the process of healthy living. As you read the following chapters, my hope is that the same becomes true for you in your relationship with Jesus.

DISCUSSION QUESTIONS

1. What do you think needs to happen after you start following Jesus?

2. What are other life examples of seeking results instead of committing to a process?

3. How can you focus on the process instead of the results when following Jesus?

4. How do we develop the "Fruit of the Spirit?"

5. Why must faith come before action?

6

HOW DO I MAKE MY RELATIONSHIP STATUS OFFICIAL?

When my wife and I started dating in college, Facebook had only been around for a short time. We were the generation that grew up on MySpace and Xanga (If you don't know what those are, Google it), so we were somewhat familiar with the concept. Still, it took a while to get used to it. As we began dating over the first few weeks, we had conversations that started to define our relationship. "Is this serious?" "Are we girlfriend/boyfriend now?" "Do we tell other people?"—you know, the usual relationship stuff. But probably the most pivotal moment in making our dating relationship official was changing our status on Facebook. It was a big choice we had to make together. After long conversations, we decided to log into Facebook and change our relationship status to "In a relationship" with each other. It was a big deal. After that, everyone knew that we were dating.

I think we were some of the first ones to go through the "Facebook Official" stage. No one even thinks twice about it now. If you are dating someone, it's not official until you put it on social media of some kind. It's the norm. But at that time, it was still pretty new for us. It's funny to think about how relationships became official before social media. Couples would tell friends and family and let them spread the word or attend a public event together. That would establish the status of your relationship.

Regardless of generation or technology, if you care about someone, it has always been important to make that relationship official. Did you know the same is true about our relationship with Jesus? Since it is the most important relationship we will develop in our lives, it is vital that we "make it official." When we start following Jesus, we cannot keep it a secret. We must begin to let other people know. Don't worry, you don't have to go stand on a street corner with a bullhorn and proclaim it to everyone. There are actually some pretty simple and easy steps we find in Scripture that allow us to go public with our relationship with Jesus.

The most common first step that we find in Scripture is baptism. There are many examples in the New Testament of baptism occurring after someone made a decision to follow Jesus. The book of Acts gives us the best account of the growth of the church after Jesus ascended into Heaven. This was the time when the church began to develop, and followers of Jesus lived out his teachings. And one of the most common things that we find in the book of Acts is someone being baptized after deciding to follow Jesus (Acts 2:38-41, Acts 19:5-6, Acts 22:16).

This is a tradition that has continued on in the church since that time. It is the clearest way that we can make a public profession of our faith, and it is a command that Jesus gave to us. Matthew 28:19 says, "Go, therefore, and make disciples of all nations, *baptizing* them in the name of the Father and of the Son and of the Holy Spirit." Baptism occurs after a genuine decision to follow Jesus. It is not necessary to be baptized more than once or each time you join a new church. When you make a decision to follow Jesus, then you should be baptized afterward. Many churches offer classes on baptism. If you have never been baptized before, I encourage you to take one of those classes, or if classes aren't available, set up a time to talk through the decision with a spiritual leader in your life.

Remember, the most essential part of baptism is making your decision to follow Jesus official. That decision is one that changes the rest of your life. Like I mentioned in previous chapters, your life is now ordered around a different set of priories, and being publicly baptized helps you to establish those priorities. It's a way of letting people know about the life that you have decided to live. It's not easy to publicly announce it because there are people in your life who may not understand. It can seem scary to step out in front of other people, but it's something that must be done. Romans 1:16 says, "For I am not ashamed of the gospel, because it is the power of God for salvation to everyone who believes." When you decide to follow Jesus, he gives you the courage and strength to boldly tell people that you are different. You cannot keep it to yourself. *Baptism is the first step in publicly declaring that your life is now different.*

In addition to baptism, it is also important to have conversations with the people you care about the most. Depending on your situation, this could mean talking with family or close friends. There will be people who are already followers of Christ, and they will be genuinely excited for you. They will encourage you and pray for you and generally be a source of support. There will also be people who do not understand, and that's ok too.

Some people do not know what it means to follow Jesus and will be skeptical of your decision. In those situations, the best thing that you can do is share your story. Don't worry if you can't quote Scripture or if you don't know everything there is to know about Christianity. Telling the people around you isn't about arguing with them or convincing them. It's more about telling your story. Give them the answers to these questions—"How did Jesus find you?" "How did he change you?" "How is your life different now?" As you tell people in your life, it will become apparent to them that Jesus is your priority now. It's a necessary step in following Jesus. You don't need to be over the top about it, but the people in your life must know about the decision you have made so that you can move forward in following Jesus.

Another vital part of public confession is the rejection of sin. Because you are now publicly professing that you follow Jesus, your life must genuinely reflect that. You can no longer live openly (or privately) in sin. There may be things in your life that you didn't realize were wrong. But, as Jesus comes into your life, he reveals to you the things that need to change. Jesus hates sin because it hurts his people in the long run. Unfortunately, when you decide to follow Jesus, sin does not magically go away. It would be much easier if we instantly became perfect, and all of our bad habits disappeared. But it does not work that way. All of us will still sin even after following Jesus.

Because we are broken people, we will continually mess up. The most significant difference is that we now have the conviction of sin and the ability to recognize when something is wrong. And we have God's promise to forgive us and give us the power to change. My encouragement is to acknowledge your brokenness, especially as you're telling the people around you. Just because you follow Jesus does not make you a perfect person. The most important thing now is admitting sin in your life and working to move past it.

There may also be some deeper issues that need to be addressed to move forward in your relationship with Jesus. Things like addictions or deeply hidden pain can be tremendous obstacles. While these two things can weigh us down, I want to make sure they aren't seen in the same category. Addictions are choices we make to bring sin into our lives. Deeply hidden pain often comes from things that happen to us or things we did not choose. One is conscious sin that we choose, and the other is something often beyond our control that happened to us. If something was done to you, you should never feel guilty that it was a choice you made even though it causes you pain.

Drug abuse, alcohol dependency, pornography, or any other perpetual sin in your life that you cannot stop is an addiction. It is challenging to stop on your own or pray them away. Deeply hidden pain like past abuse or traumatic experiences are complicated things that take hold in your life and make you feel trapped. And like addictions, you cannot let go on your own or pray the pain away. These issues may require more than just personal prayer. You may need guidance from a spiritual leader or a professional counselor to work through these, and there is nothing wrong with that. We are not meant to go through these things alone or overcome them on our own. And it may take a long time to move past them.

If you are going through any of these things, I encourage you to find someone in your life that you trust and talk with them. You do not have to go and tell everyone, but you should tell someone. *Things that are in the dark can only find healing when they are brought into the light.* Addictions and deeply hidden pain are chains that hold us down, but those chains can be broken. This is a painful thing, but it's also a good thing. Jesus sets us free from sin and pain. They still exist in our lives, but we do not carry them on our own. Even though we can never forget them, we can find the freedom to move past them. Rejecting sin and dealing with our pain allows us to truly accept the freedom that Christ gives. "Therefore, there is now no condemnation for those in Christ Jesus, because the law of the Spirit of life in Christ Jesus has set you free from the law of sin and death." (Romans 8:1-2)

When we talk about rejecting sin, it's natural to want a list. We ask questions like these—"What is right?" "What is wrong?" "What can I do?" "What can I not do?" The Bible is our best source for truth. We do find clear instructions on things that are right and wrong, and as you read it, you should take those instructions to heart. But I'm not going to give you a list of what is right and what is wrong. It's not really about that. Christianity that revolves around a list of things that you can and can't do misses the point. It becomes more about following the rules rather than following Jesus. There are lists in the Bible that talk about good things and bad things (eg. Exodus 20:1-17, Galatians 5:19-22), but each of these lists has more to do with holiness, not merely following the rules.

So when it comes to rejecting sin, instead of giving you a list, I want to encourage you to focus on following Jesus. If you are dedicated to following him and living his way, you will not need a list. He will show you what is right and what is wrong. (The following chapters describe how he shows us.) That way, your actions will come out of the joy of following him and not the obligation of obeying a set of rules. As you do that, it will become apparent to you what needs to change in your life and what needs to stay the same. And when it happens that way, the changes you make won't be done out of an obligation to follow a rule. They will be done out of love and the desire to be more like Jesus. You will know right from wrong because of the presence of the Holy Spirit in your life. And, "What is the Holy Spirit?" you ask. Follow me to the next chapter, I'll tell you.

DISCUSSION QUESTIONS

1. How do you make your relationship status with Jesus "official?"

2. Have you been baptized? If yes, when and where? If no, is it a step you're considering?

3. Why is it sometimes difficult to tell others about a decision to follow Jesus?

4. Why must things in the dark be exposed to light to find healing?

5. How does following Jesus (rather than simply following a list of rules) help you reject sin?

7

IS THE HOLY SPIRIT A GHOST?

Have you ever seen the movie, *Pinocchio*? I looked it up, and the original cartoon came out in 1940... 1940! I don't know why, but I never thought the movie was that old. There's a character in the film named Jiminy Cricket. He is appointed to be Pinocchio's conscience by the fairy that gives Pinocchio life. Throughout the movie, Jiminy Cricket is a guide on Pinocchio's quest to become a real boy. He is the voice in Pinocchio's ear, which tells him what is right and what is wrong. And he stays with Pinocchio even when he makes the wrong choice. He is generally the guiding force in Pinocchio's life. When we think about the Holy Spirit, this is often the image that comes to mind. The most common perception is something like Jiminy Cricket or a devil on one shoulder and an angel on the other trying to tell us what to do. This comparison isn't totally wrong, but it's definitely not totally right.

The Holy Spirit is so much more than a voice in our ear that tells us what to do. The Holy Spirit *IS* God. The Bible tells us that God is Father, Son, and Spirit; three in one and one in three. It's a concept that can make our brains hurt. Still, the idea that God is all three simultaneously without being separate is an essential truth of our faith. Usually, the Holy Spirit is the least talked about of these three, but the Holy Spirit is God, just like God the Father and Jesus the Son. He is not just a voice in our ear that gives us a conscience. *The Holy Spirit is God himself, actively participating in our lives.*

The Holy Spirit has existed as God himself since the beginning of time. There are many references in the Old Testament to the Spirit of God. (Genesis 1:2, Psalm 139:7, Exodus 31: 3). This shows us that it has always been God's desire to be present with his people. But it wasn't until after Jesus ascended into Heaven that the Holy Spirit came to live in each follower of Jesus individually. This was God's way of fulfilling his promise to always be with us. The Holy Spirit is God with us just as Jesus was God with his disciples during his time on earth. Because of what Jesus did, the Holy Spirit came fully into our lives, and we now have access to God through his presence.

It is crucial to establish that the Holy Spirit is God before discussing the roles he plays in our lives. If we see him as anything else, we will be vastly underestimating his presence. He is not a ghost. He is not a conscience. He is not a mythical spirit. He *IS* God. Are we clear on that? Cool, let's keep going. There are several roles that the Holy Spirit plays in our lives, and the best description we have for those roles comes from the Bible. Let's take a look at a few of these to see how the Holy Spirit functions.

"And I will ask the Father, and he will give you another Counselor to be with you forever. He is the Spirit of truth. The world is unable to receive him because it doesn't see him or know him. But you do know him, because he remains with you and will be in you." (John 14:16-17)

This is Jesus talking. He said these words the night before he was crucified when he was giving final instructions to his disciples. They didn't fully understand what was about to happen, but Jesus knew that they would look back on these words for guidance. Jesus is telling them that even though he will leave, God will still be with them through the Holy Spirit. Before this time, the people of God had to go to the temple and use the priest to access God's presence. Jesus is saying that will no longer be necessary. Because of the work that he was about to do, everyone could now be in God's presence at any time, through the Holy Spirit. He also refers to the Holy Spirit as the "Counselor." I love that description.

Another way of describing it would be an advocate or a helping presence like a legal counselor. I don't know about you, but life is complicated for me, and it's often difficult to know what is right and what is wrong. Having access to a "Counselor" is a fantastic gift!

He shows us how to live. He counsels us through every situation. Jesus also says that he convicts us of sin. When we do mess up, he is the one who convicts us and points us toward what is right. He helps us navigate this complicated and messy life. We won't always get it right, but when we don't, he is there to help get us back on course.

"I still have many things to tell you, but you can't bear them now. When the Spirit of truth comes, he will guide you into all the truth. For he will not speak on his own, but he will speak whatever he hears. He will also declare to you what is to come. He will glorify me, because he will take from what is mine and declare it to you." (John 16:12-14)

A few verses later, Jesus goes on to say that the Holy Spirit will also act as a guide for us. He will guide us into truth. During Jesus' life, he gave us incredible teaching to follow. Because life is so complex, we don't necessarily have specific instructions for every situation that we could face. It would be nice if we had specific instructions that tell us what to do in every circumstance.

But we actually have something better. In the Bible, we find Jesus' teachings that give us truth to order our lives around. The Holy Spirit provides us with the wisdom to live out and apply that truth in each unique circumstance. With Scripture and the Holy Spirit together, we have everything we need to live God's way. Both of these things work together, and they will never contradict each other. If your conscience tells you to do something contrary to the Bible's teachings, that is not the Holy Spirit. The Bible gives us truth. The Holy Spirit provides us with the wisdom to act out that truth in every situation. They will always land in agreement with one another. The Holy Spirit is our guide in life. He is the one that we depend on to show us the way. But unlike Jiminy Crickett, he is not someone trying their best to tell us what's right. He is God himself, showing us his will.

"When the day of Pentecost had arrived, they were all together in one place. Suddenly a sound like that of a violent rushing wind came from Heaven, and it filled the whole house where they were staying. They saw tongues like flames of fire that separated and rested on each one of them. Then they were all filled with the Holy Spirit and began to speak in different tongues, as the Spirit enabled them." (Acts 2:1-4)

If there was any doubt that Jesus' words would come true, this passage in Acts shows how the Holy Spirit came upon the followers of Jesus. After Jesus died, rose again, and ascended into Heaven, the disciples were waiting together. They had seen Jesus rise from the dead, but they were still uncertain about what was next. This event is important because it is a powerful moment that shows how the Holy Spirit will be present to all followers of Christ until Jesus returns. This event set the tone for the early followers of Jesus. It gave them the courage and boldness to begin living out Jesus' teachings.

Even though Jesus had ascended to Heaven, they were not alone. God was with them through the presence of his Spirit. They faced persecution and many difficult circumstances, but they lived them all with joy and boldness because the Holy Spirit was there to guide them. Even though that happened two thousand years ago, we can do the same today. Jesus is not physically with us, but we are not alone. God's presence is in our lives through his Spirit, just like it was for the early followers of Jesus.

"In the same way the Spirit also helps us in our weakness, because we do not know what to pray for as we should, but the Spirit himself intercedes for us with inexpressible groanings. And he who searches our hearts knows the mind of the Spirit, because he intercedes for the saints according to the will of God." (Romans 8:26-27)

"Intercede" is a fancy word (or a ten-dollar word as my grandpa used to say), but it is an important one. It means to intervene on someone's behalf by praying for them. These verses are some of the most comforting to me. This is where the "advocate" or "legal counselor" part of his description comes into play. There are times in our lives where we feel so at a loss that we don't even know what to do, what to say, or even how to pray. It could be a difficult situation. It could be pain or suffering. It could be a recognition of sin in our lives or many other painful things. Whatever the case is, when these times happen, we might feel like God wants nothing to do with us or is far away. We don't know how to pray, or if we did, we don't even know what we would say to him.

When we feel confused and lost like this, the Holy Spirit intercedes for us. Read that again. It's amazing! When we can't pray, the Holy Spirit prays for us! When God feels far away, the Holy Spirit connects us to him. God loves us so much that even when we can't do any of these things, the Holy Spirit does it for us. That is one of the most comforting things in the world to me. It's ok that I don't have the right words or the perfect attitude in difficult times. It's ok when I'm hurting or broken. It's ok when I don't know what to say. The Holy Spirit connects me to God through "inexpressible groanings." He is my words when I don't have them. He is my strength when I am weak. He prays for me when I can't. Because of the Holy Spirit, God is always with us.

"Don't you know that your body is a temple of the Holy Spirit who is in you, whom you have from God?" (1 Corinthians 6:19)

This is the last verse that I want to share with you about the Holy Spirit because I think it gives us the best understanding of how to live our lives with the knowledge of his presence. When we really understand who he is, we start to see that instead of inviting him into our lives, it's more about him asking us to be a part of God's kingdom. Our bodies and our lives are not our own. This world is not our own. All of these things are gifts from God, and we are invited to live as part of his kingdom.

Our priority becomes living for him and not for ourselves. Isn't it amazing to realize that if you are a follower of Jesus, the Spirit of God lives inside of you? Like the early followers of Jesus, you get to live out God's will right where you are. Because the Holy Spirit lives in you, you can have the courage and wisdom to act in every situation. You get to participate in God's kingdom here on earth. As you live that way, you will become more and more like Jesus.

In Chapter 5, I talked about the fruit of the Spirit. We saw how important it is to follow Jesus first so that fruit will be present (love, joy, peace, patience, kindness, goodness, faithfulness, gentleness, and self-control). I want to repeat that here. Don't focus on the fruit. Focus on following Jesus. As you recognize the Holy Spirit's presence in your life, you will begin to see these fruits naturally. You will not have to try to be good or kind. It will happen naturally as the Spirit guides you. Listening to the Spirit is the best way to develop the habits and traits needed to follow Jesus.

So how do we recognize the Holy Spirit and communicate with him? It's important to start with the knowledge about the Holy Spirit, but I want to move toward the practical side of things. How do we experience the Holy Spirit every day? The most practical ways that we experience him are through spiritual habits. Spiritual habits are practices we develop in order to deepen our relationship with God. There are many spiritual habits that can be learned as we move forward in our relationship with Jesus. However, because this book is about starting from the beginning, these are the three habits to start with when learning how to experience the Holy Spirit— (1) Prayer, (2) Scripture, and (3) godly friendships... Guess what the next three chapters are about?

DISCUSSION QUESTIONS

1. How have you viewed the Holy Spirit in the past?

2. Why is it so important to believe that the Holy Spirit is God?

3. How does the Holy Spirit act as a "Counselor?"

4. Why is it important to believe that the Holy Spirit will not contradict something found in the Bible?

5. In what situation might the Holy Spirit "intercede" on your behalf?

8

IS IT POSSIBLE TO HAVE A CONVERSATION WITH GOD?

In 1962, scientists from Russia sent the first message into outer space to communicate with extra-terrestrial life. Since then, numerous attempts have been made to send messages into space. Some messages were sent in good fun; some were sent merely to prove that we have the technology to do it. Others were sent sincerely looking to communicate with life in outer space. I've seen enough alien movies (Independence Day, ET, Men In Black, etc...) to feel a bit nervous about this. There are very few movies where aliens show up with good intentions. In most of the films, the aliens show up with a fleet of warships prepared to destroy earth. Somehow, the hero always saves the day, but it's usually after quite a bit of death and destruction. I'm not saying I believe in aliens. However, if they did exist, these messages broadcasting earth's location might not be the best idea. I don't think Will Smith could save us from aliens in real life.

One thing these messages to outer space have in common is that they were sent without any certainty that they would be received. They were transmitted, hoping that something might happen. When I first started praying, this is how I felt. My prayers felt like hopeful transmissions to outer space without any certainty that someone was on the other end listening. I don't think I'm the only one that has ever viewed prayer that way. In fact, I think all of us either still feel that way or have felt that way in the past. But because of the Holy Spirit, not only can we communicate directly with God, we can also develop a real relationship with him just as we would a close friend. The Holy Spirit gives us the certainty that our prayers are not only heard, but God is actively participating in our lives through a relationship with us.

Communication is fundamental to any relationship. In my marriage relationship, when I do not work on communication, it leads to frustration and a feeling of distance. For example, one of the hardest times in our marriage was when I spent time training in a different city for a new job. We had to spend a lot of time apart from one another. I'm not a big fan of talking on the phone, but I did my best to spend time talking with my wife. We were able to see each other occasionally, but we felt disconnected and far away. A lack of communication and time together hurt our relationship. It really taught us how important it is to communicate well and spend time with one another. And since that time, we have tried our best not to go through situations like that again.

In the same way, when I do not work on my communication with God, it leads to a feeling of frustration and distance from him. Many people would say that God feels far away. When that happens, we must ask ourselves, "What am I doing to communicate?" "Am I doing my part?" If we never spend time praying, it makes a lot of sense that God would feel far away.

He desires to be a part of our lives and to have a relationship with us. Instead of seeing our relationship with him as him being our master or some stern authority figure, the Bible tells us to view him as our Father. I know that term is not helpful for everyone. Some people have grown up without a father or with a father who was not kind to them. But true fatherhood was not designed to be that way. When the Bible describes God as a Father, it is meant in the most perfect way. He is a Father who loves us more than we can imagine. He is a Father who cares deeply about how we are doing and what's happening in our lives. He is a Father who is there for us no matter what. He is a Father who defends us and fights for us. He is the perfect Father. That is who we are praying to and developing a relationship with.

When we see God as our Father, it helps lessen the intimidation of prayer. If we see God as a stern master or threatening authority figure, it keeps us from praying. We feel like we have to be perfect or clean up our lives before we can pray. We feel like he will judge us or think less of us because of our mistakes. But that could not be further from the truth. God is our loving Father who accepts us just as we are, mistakes and all.

When we pray, we can do so with the freedom to be honest in every way. We can tell him that we have messed up and ask for forgiveness. We can say that we are angry at him or emotional about difficult things in our lives. We can ask him questions when doubt creeps in. Not only can he handle it all, but he loves our honesty because it builds intimacy and trust with him. Imperfect, messy prayers are the best place to start.

A common question about prayer is, "Does prayer even make a difference?" Another way of saying this is, "Can prayer actually change things?" If we cannot control what happens in life, does prayer even matter? While it is impossible for us to fully know God's mind and how he works, prayer matters so much. The key here is that *prayer is not about changing God or changing circumstances; prayer is mainly about changing us.*

If God is perfect, would we rather have our way or his way? When we pray and ask for things, the best thing that can happen is to learn how to see the situation the way he does. This means that we will often change what we are asking. John 15:7 says, "If you remain in me and my words remain in you, ask whatever you want, and it will be done for you." We like to jump to the last part of this verse—we can ask for whatever we want, and he will do it for us! If we just focused on that part of the verse, we would treat God like a genie granting wishes. "I want to win the lottery!" "I want a better job!" "I want more happiness in life!" But we cannot miss the first part of that verse. "If you remain in me and my words remain in you..."

If we are indeed developing a relationship with God and learning to live our lives his way, the things we ask for will change. We would not ask to win the lottery because we realize that money cannot buy true joy. Instead, we would ask for the joy that can only come from God. We would care about the things that God cares about—the things that really matter. We might ask God to meet our needs for sure, but we will also ask for a generous heart and the opportunity to give to others in need.

We should pray and ask God for things. We should tell him about our hurts and difficulties. We should ask for his help. But as we do, we must realize that prayer changes us more than it changes God, and that's a good thing. It is not about getting our way or getting him to change our situation. It is about learning to see our lives the way that he sees it. And the best part is, his way is so much better than ours.

If you can't tell by now, one of my pet peeves is knowledge without practical application. So, practically, how do we pray each day? Set an appointment to meet God every day. When we care about someone, we make time to get to know them better and cherish them as part of our lives. We make them a priority by saying "No" to other things in order to create more time. The same is true for our relationship with God. The "No" of denying other things leads to a "Yes" of spending time with God. If we do not plan for time in prayer, it will not happen very often. Other things, sometimes good things, will always get in the way. But even good things can get in the way of the best thing. We must create time for prayer each day, even if it's just a few minutes at first. It should not be done as an obligation but as a joyful act of spending time with someone we love.

When we pray, there is no need to get something out of it or to accomplish anything. The most important thing is to just be with God. Because of the Holy Spirit, you can trust that he is there with you. As you pray, you can honestly tell God what is going on in your life, but you should also make time to listen. He has things to say to you as well. He often communicates to us through his Word (the Bible) or through our thoughts inspired by the Holy Spirit. You should pray for others and about things that are bothering you. You should also ask for things. But we should also learn to thank God for the good things in our lives and praise him for who he is.

Imagine if you had a friend that only came to you with the bad stuff and dumped it on you. You wouldn't like that friend. We should not treat God that way. He is a great listener and we should tell him everything. But he wants to share in all of it, not just the bad stuff. Sometimes when you pray, words will not be spoken, and that's ok. Prayer doesn't always need words. Make time to be with him every day, and over time it will begin to change you in some beautiful ways.

You may also have times where you pray out loud with others. This is usually one of the most terrifying things for people who have never done it before. You are afraid that you will say the wrong thing, or people will judge you for not being "good" at prayer. These are common fears, but do not give into them. Praying in front of other people is not about trying to impress them or prove something to them. Praying out loud with others is about a few people having a conversation with the Lord together.

Praying with others can be weird and awkward at first, but it is a good thing and does not stay weird and awkward. This might happen in your family or in groups of friends who are also followers of Christ. If you are among people who love Jesus, they will joyfully join you in group communication with the Father. They will not care how articulate you are or how "good" you are at praying. Just talk to God with other people.

If you ever find yourself praying so that other people will hear you, reset your perspective, and speak only to God. Matthew 6:5 says, "Whenever you pray, you must not be like the hypocrites, because they love to pray standing in the synagogues and on the street corners to be seen by people. Truly I tell you, they have their reward." When we let go of trying to impress others, prayer in a group becomes a beautiful thing.

As you pray consistently, you will also begin to develop another type of prayer with realizing it. 1 Thessalonians 5:17 says, "Pray constantly." It is a short but powerful verse. How do we pray constantly? How could we spend an entire day praying? Would we ever get anything else done? This verse helps us understand that prayer does not only happen when we bow our heads and close our eyes. Prayer can happen at any time and in any place.

When you pray regularly, you will begin to notice changes in your everyday life. The presence of God will be with you in every situation, and you will feel his guidance in the small daily things. This is not God, finally being present in your life. He is and has always been there. This is you becoming more aware of his presence. As you realize that, it leads to prayer happening deep below the surface.

While we may not be praying out loud or directly with words in our minds, we are in tune with God's presence. Deep inside of us, the Holy Spirit is maintaining constant prayer with him on our behalf. We do not leave God when we leave our set time of prayer each day. Being with him is not a switch that we turn on and off. Set times of prayer set the tone for each day and help us to recognize that his presence goes with us no matter what. This is what it means to pray constantly. As we learn and grow, it becomes a natural part of who we are.

There is no secret formula to prayer, but there is growth. Prayer will get better and easier the more you do it. It is important to measure your growth in years (long-term) and not days or weeks (short-term). You have your entire life to pray. Don't worry if prayer is still difficult in just a few weeks or if you regress in some way. Prayer takes time to learn—a lot of time.

Healthy marriages are usually marriages that have spent years and years learning how to communicate well. In the same way, our communication with God will get better after years and years of practice. Instead of looking back to see how far you have come in a few weeks, look back in a few years. Real growth happens over long periods, and since prayer is not a race, that's a good thing. Many more levels of prayer will become apparent to you as you grow deeper in your relationship with God.

The most important thing to remember is that prayer is not just something you do. It's someone you're with. When you see it that way, it takes the pressure off. You do not have to be perfect. You do not have to achieve or earn something, and you do not have doubt that you are heard and valued. When you pray, you are not like the scientists who tentatively sent messages into space, hoping someone would listen. Because of the Holy Spirit, you can pray to someone who is already with you. He hears you and cares about what you have to say. When you pray, you get to be present with someone— your Heavenly Father, who loves you more than you can ever imagine.

DISCUSSION QUESTIONS

1. How is it possible to have a conversation with God?

2. Why is communication important in any relationship?

3. Why do you think God desires to communicate with us?

4. Why should prayer change you?

5. Why is it difficult to listen during prayer?

9

THE BIBLE IS SUCH A BIG BOOK... DO I HAVE TO READ IT?

Pizza is the only reason I know how to read. When I was in First Grade, my school participated in something called "The Pizza Hut Book It Program." Our teacher would set a reading goal, and, if we achieved it, we got a coupon for a free kid's pizza. At that time, my family rarely went out to eat. My mom and dad worked hard to provide for us, but as small business owners with four (hungry) kids, eating out wasn't a regular option. So when my school started this reading program, I was highly motivated to get free pizza. I read every book we had at school and at home. I read every book I could find. I read so much that I think the teacher ran out of pizza coupons.

Make no mistake, though. I was not reading to further my education or improve my reading skills. I was reading for pizza. But while I was eating all of that free pizza, something happened. I actually became a good reader. More than that, I secretly began to like reading. I started off only caring about pizza. But over time, I really began to enjoy reading, and that benefit stuck with me.

I'm here to tell you that if you start reading the Bible, you will get free pizza... just kidding! Sometimes we need the right motivation to do something that doesn't come naturally for us. Some of you may love reading, and the idea of reading the Bible sounds like a great idea. But I suspect many people fall into the category of not enjoying reading or being intimidated by the Bible. And that's ok. It's a really big book. But this really big book contains God's story and truth for his people.

Reading it is how we learn who God is and how much he loves us. Reading it shows us what it means to follow Jesus and gives us the principles to live that way today. Reading it allows the Holy Spirit to provide communication with the Father through his Word. That is way better than free pizza. The good news is you don't have to read it all at once, and there is no rush or deadline to finish it all. We have our entire lives to read and study the Bible. The point isn't to finish it so that we can pridefully say that we've read it. *Reading the Bible is about letting the Holy Spirit speak to us and connect us closer to the heart of God.*

Before I give you some practical instructions on how to read the Bible, I want to briefly tell you where it came from and why we trust that it is true. The Bible is comprised of 66 books and two sections—the Old

Testament (39 books) and the New Testament (27 books). God made covenants with his people, and each "testament" is an account of God's people living under those covenants. The Old Testament established the covenant of The Law of Moses. It looked forward to its ultimate fulfillment in the new covenant.

The New Testament established the new covenant of freedom in Christ and a personal relationship with the Father. Each book either documented history or sent words from the Lord to others, and they were written by people who followed God. 2 Timothy 3:16-17 says, "All Scripture is inspired by God and is profitable for teaching, for rebuking, for correcting, for training in righteousness, so that the man of God may be complete, equipped for every good work." The Bible was written by God's Spirit, working through human authors. This is why we often refer to the Bible as "God's Word."

Bible scholars try hard to know who wrote what book and why because it helps us better understand that book and how it fits into God's Story. We mostly know who wrote what book and why. However, the author/intention of some books is up for debate because they were written a long time ago. And we don't have all the information we would like to have about the situation. Genesis is the first book in the Old Testament. It starts with the story of how God created the world. Revelation is the last book in the New Testament. It gives a glimpse of how God will one day restore his creation and establish Heaven on earth. Everything in between tells God's Story for his people.

Because the account of the Old Testament starts at the beginning of time and ends several hundred years before the time of Jesus, we don't know exactly how it was put together. We know that in its current form, it was preserved for hundreds of years by Jewish leaders and scribes. Scribes were people whose job was to handwrite texts to preserve them. It was written in Hebrew, which was the language of the Jews. Godly leaders in the Jewish community were able to discern which books needed to be designated as God's Word. Before the time of Jesus, the Old Testament was the Bible and the only source of truth for God's people. It was revered and used by God's people to know God's story and to find righteousness.

By the time of Jesus, The Old Testament had been collected into mostly the same format that we have today. It might seem obvious, but we have to remind ourselves that all Jesus and his followers had was the Old Testament. The version that we read today has been translated many times over the years from Hebrew into many different languages, including the language I'm using now, English. The Old Testament describes the first part of the story that we saw in Chapter 2—the entry of sin and brokenness into the world. And it is also full of God's promises to restore his people.[1]

The New Testament starts with the book of Matthew. It tells the story of how Jesus came into this world and established God's plan for his people. It also describes how God's people formed the early church in order to establish Jesus' teachings as a way of life. We know a lot more about how the New Testament came together because it happened within the last 2,000 years, and we have much better historical accounts. At that time, the common language was an ancient form of Greek known as Koine ("common") Greek. All versions of The New Testament that we read today were originally written in Koine Greek.

Within 100 years after Jesus died, rose again, and ascended into Heaven, several books had already come together. Matthew, Mark, Luke and John (The Gospels) and the letters of Paul, an important leader in the early church, were already in circulation. These books were generally accepted as authoritative books of the Bible by followers of Christ. After that, leaders in the church worked to recognize which books should be included and which ones should not. Several books were circulating that didn't meet their standards. By the end of the 4th century A.D., they were able to establish a set of criteria, based on the truths of Jesus' teachings, to discern which books were worthy of being designated as God's Word.[2]

I do not want to get bogged down in the history of the Bible, but I think it's essential to have a basic understanding of how it came together. We should not just read it blindly. We should be confident that it is true. We should be confident that the Holy Spirit, working through godly leaders, painstakingly put it together and preserved it for followers of Jesus to use over the centuries.

I encourage you to do more study on your own. There are many great (and not great) resources that explain how the Bible was preserved and the process that we use to confirm its authenticity. Leaders in your local church should be able to point you toward helpful and trustworthy tools. Because it was written so long ago, we don't have every answer, and we don't know everything there is to know. Despite all that, there is so much we do know that scholars and historians have worked hard to preserve. We can have confidence today that the Bible is God's words for us.

Practically speaking, there are a few things to know about reading the Bible. First, the English Bible that we use has many different translations. Each translation was carefully formed by Bible and language scholars. They started with the Koine Greek and translated it verse by verse into English. As you can imagine, each translation is different. Translators have different audiences in mind, and they make translations for various reasons. Languages are also very different. Often you do not have one word in a language that corresponds to that exact word in the Greek text. While translating, scholars also have to take into account the culture and context of the people in the world of the Bible as well as the context of the people they are translating for. Bridging the gap between "then" and "now" can be quite a challenge.

Some translations try very hard to give word-for-word accounts of the original text. These translations can be challenging to read because word-for-word language translation is difficult. Think of it this way. If you are to translate word-for-word the Spanish phrase "Me gusta

Taco Bell," in English, it would be "Taco Bell pleases me." It is word-for-word accurate but not the most efficient or even accurate way to communicate. It would be more comfortable and better to just say, "I like Taco Bell." (I really do like Taco Bell and don't judge me for it.) For that reason, some translations focus more on giving the idea of each text. These translations are usually easier to read but may not always use the exact words that we find in the original language. This is why there are so many different translations in English (and other languages).

People have approached the translation process with different intentions and goals. While each one is different, almost all of them adhere to sound biblical truth. Throughout this book, I have used the same translation, the Christian Standard Bible (CSB). In addition to the CSB, I also recommend the New International Version (NIV), the New English Translation (NET), or the New Living Translation (NLT) for first time Bible readers. These are easy to read versions that also provide accurate translations.

Once you decide on a translation, the next step is to determine how you will most enjoy reading it. Because of modern technology, we have several ways that we can read the Bible. There are physical copies of the Bible that you can read. These can be found in bookstores or online. Some people prefer to actually hold and feel a book in their hands while reading it.

There are also digital copies of the Bible. These can be found on platforms like Kindle, iBooks, Google

Books, and many more. Several apps can be used on almost any device. YouVersion is a great free choice that contains hundreds of translations.

Another popular way to read is through audiobooks. Some people prefer to listen to a book because they either comprehend better or have more time on commutes or other jobs to listen. YouVersion has an audio option on its app. Also, a quick google search of "Audio Bible" will give many great choices. The important thing is that you choose what works for you. Everyone reads and comprehends differently. However you read it, you can know that it will be beneficial to you.

Once you decide what and how you are going to read, the hardest part comes into play—actually doing it! Because the Bible is such a big book, it is intimidating and seems impossible to read. I encourage you not to take the mindset that it's an assignment that you have to complete. Instead, see it as a way of letting the Holy Spirit reveal himself to you. You are not reading it to make someone happy or because you're obligated to read it. You're reading because it will grow your faith and give you a better understanding of who God is.

When you start reading, start slow. Go for quality over quantity. It is better to read and reflect on two verses that influence your life than to read two books and remember nothing. You have your whole life to read it, so there is no rush to make it all the way through in a set amount of time. It's not a race! Just make sure you are reading it consistently. Make time for it as a regular habit, even if it's just a few minutes a day.

Start with the New Testament. Read about the life of Jesus in one of the four Gospels and how the early church lived after Jesus left in the book of Acts. Once you make it through the New Testament, move to the Old Testament. Read about how God created the world and established his people. In addition to finding truth, you will also find some pretty crazy and fascinating stories. The Bible is not a bland book. Over time you will read substantial portions of the Bible without realizing it. And because it is such a big book, it will never get old. If you ever finish all of it, it will not be hard to return to it often and continue reading parts that you have read before. In fact, reading for the second, third, or fourth time often reveals something we did not see the first time.

When reading the Bible, I would also recommend finding someone you trust to answer any questions you have. You will come across things that may be hard to understand or may not make sense. Find a reliable spiritual leader to discuss these questions. No one has all the answers to every question, but wise, mature people can help answer some of your questions. You may even consider finding a group of people with whom you can study the Bible together. This is a great way to read the Bible. Different people reading it, experiencing it, and discussing it together can lead to great conversations and understanding.

We cannot neglect reading the Bible. When I talked about the Holy Spirit in Chapter 7, I gave three ways that God communicates with us. One of those ways was reading Scripture. If this is a meaningful way that God speaks to us, we must take it seriously. We cannot let excuses or the intimidation of reading a big book get in the way. "For the word of God is living and effective and sharper than any double-edged sword, penetrating as far as the separation of soul and spirit, joints and marrow. It is able to judge the thoughts and intentions of the heart." (Hebrews 4:12)

God's Word is a foundational part of our faith. It is just as relevant today as it was thousands of years ago. God's truth is so powerful that it transcends culture, language, and context. For centuries, the people of God have read it, studied it, and reflected on it to experience God in a powerful, life-changing way. You can do the same. And the reward for reading it is so much better than free pizza.

DISCUSSION QUESTIONS

1. Why is the Bible so intimidating to read?

2. How does the Holy Spirit speak to us through the Bible?

3. Why can we trust that the Bible is God's Word?

4. What is your favorite method to read (physical book, digital, audio, etc…)?

5. How can you start reading the Bible regularly?

10

DO I NEED FRIENDS WHO ALSO FOLLOW JESUS?

I love to cook. I joke with my family that I am a chef disguised as a pastor. I love to cook because I love to eat, and the two pretty much go hand in hand. Over the years of cooking, I have learned how vital salt is. You have probably eaten food that is too salty and food that is not salty enough. Both too much and too little salt make food less enjoyable. When you eat foods with the best flavor, it usually means they have the right amount of salt. In addition to adding flavor, salt is also a preservative. Before modern refrigeration, people used to preserve meat and other foods through salt. Unrefrigerated foods will spoil without salt.

"You are the salt of the earth. But if the salt should lose its taste, how can it be made salty? It's no longer good for anything but to be thrown out and trampled under people's feet." (Matthew 5:13)

Salt is also biblical! The chef part of me is very excited about that. In this verse, it's not referring to salt as a flavoring. It's referring to salt as a preservative.[3] So when Jesus says to his followers, "You are the salt of the earth," he is saying that you are the ones tasked with preserving God's kingdom on earth. Just like salt preserves meat to keep it from spoiling, so we, the Church, are supposed to preserve God's kingdom from being spoiled by anything other than his way and his teachings. We do this first by finding our identity only in him. And second, we do this by bonding with fellow believers both locally and globally to live out his Heaven-minded mission here on earth.

You do not need salt to live. You can eat food without salt and still get the nourishment you need to sustain life. In the same way, you can live without friends. You do not need a community to survive. But when you live in community with other followers of Jesus, it preserves your life, just like salt preserves your food. Godly friendships keep you from going astray, just like salt keeps food from spoiling. Living in community brings so much joy and support in life, and it makes us better versions of ourselves. *Godly friendships encourage us, point us toward truth, and give us direction from the Holy Spirit.*

Finding friends who follow Jesus might make you realize that some of your current friendships are not good.

This is a painful realization. You don't always have to stop being friends with those people, but you need to do some serious self-reflection. Are those friends influencing you to be more like Jesus or less like Jesus? Unfortunately, our parents and teachers were right growing up. You become like the company you keep.

Now that following Jesus is the priority in your life, you must make sure that the people who are influencing you are pointing you in the right direction. You don't have to stop being friends with people who aren't followers of Jesus. You just have to stop letting them influence you. This is a hard step, and your friends will not always understand. They might even criticize you or ridicule you. There is no need to argue with them or pridefully pretend that you are better than them. Instead, in humility, share with them that you still love them and that Jesus is now the one who sets priorities in your life. You can no longer participate in everything they do. Your life is different now.

The first step in finding godly friendships is finding a local church. Unfortunately, churches have been painted as hypocritical, out of touch places. While this may be true of a few, there are great churches everywhere that can enhance your life. Churches are full of imperfect people trying their best to follow Jesus. Because none of us are perfect, there will be times when we, as followers of Jesus, act like hypocrites. My advice is to you is this— don't look for a perfect church. They don't exist. Instead, look for a church that knows it isn't perfect and is striving to follow Jesus..

Because there are so many denominations and different types of churches, it can be tough to give specific advice here. Instead of a long list of things to do, I encourage you to start with this—look for a church that is both centered on Biblical teaching and loving others. Some churches can lean toward one or the other. A church that cares more about truth than love will often be seen as judgmental and uncaring. On the flip side, a church that cares more about love than truth will often lack accountability for sin. Jesus has called us to do both—truth AND love! Find a church that does both.

As the Holy Spirit becomes a stronger part of your life, he will guide you toward the right church. You will know what is true and right based on your personal prayer and study of the Bible. Because of that, you will know which church you need to be a part of. You will find a church that humbly admits its faults and genuinely expresses its desire to point people toward Jesus.

When you find a church, it is important to participate in what we call "corporate worship." This means a regular gathering of a group of people to pray, hear biblical teaching, and sing praises to God. You could live on your own without this, but like food without salt, you will not preserve your relationship with Jesus well. It makes following Jesus better. We were not created to live alone. God created us to live in community! We find so many examples in the Bible of the followers of Jesus gathering together to find strength and support as they sought to live like Jesus. Encouraging one another to follow Jesus is an important aspect of the local church.

"And let us consider how we may spur one another on toward love and good deeds, not giving up meeting together, as some are in the habit of doing, but encouraging one another—and all the more as you see the Day approaching." (Hebrews 10:24-25)

As you participate in corporate worship, it is also helpful to find friends that can become a regular part of your life. Large gatherings are necessary, but on their own, they are not enough to give us healthy relationships. It is also good to find a smaller circle of friends you can spend time with regularly. This circle does not always have to include only people from your local church. The standard for that circle of friends should be that they are also followers of Jesus. This smaller circle of people can be an incredible foundation of strength, encouragement, and wisdom. Imagine having friends who loved you no matter what and told you the truth even when you didn't want to hear it? We all need that. The Holy Spirit speaks to us through friendships like these.

This does not mean that you shouldn't have friendships with people who aren't followers of Jesus. That is not the example that Jesus set for us. He spent time with everyone, regardless of who they were. What we do learn from his life is that we have different circles. In his book, *A Spirituality of Living*, Henry Nouwen gives us a great breakdown of the example that Jesus set for us. Jesus had "solitude" with God, "community" with his disciples, and "ministry" with everyone around him.

Our solitude with God is the personal relationship we develop with him that is the foundation of who we are. Our community with others is our participation in the local church and the close circle of friendships with other followers of Jesus. This community provides us strength and encouragement to live like Jesus. Our ministry is the relationships we develop with people who aren't followers of Jesus. Because of our solitude and our community, we can confidently develop friendships with anyone. Jesus did it, and so can we.

We should not live in isolation only with other believers. On the night before he died, Jesus prayed these words over his disciples "I am not praying that you take them out of the world but that you protect them from the evil one. They are not of the world, just as I am not of the world. Sanctify them by the truth; your word is truth. As you sent me into the world, I also have sent them into the world." (John 17:15-18) Jesus has not called us to isolate ourselves from this world. We should not run from it or separate ourselves from it even if the world doesn't act as we do. We actively participate in it by living like Jesus. And as we do that, people will see there is something different about us.

Your relationship with God and your friendships with other believers provide the support you need to go out and live like Jesus without compromising who you are. It is not an easy thing to do because it will go against the norm. Our culture does not understand the teachings of Jesus. Denying yourself, putting others first, and loving your enemies are not popular things to do.

Because of that, we need support from people who are doing the same. As we do that, we can go out confidently and proclaim who Jesus is both by what we say and by what we do.

One last note about community—We must realize that no matter what country we live in, we are part of a broader community of believers throughout the world and throughout history. We are not American Christians. We are Christians who live in America. This is why I started the book by talking about how I like terms like "follower of Jesus" better than "Christian." In our culture, "Christian" often means "American Christian" and not "follower of Jesus." There is a difference. Don't hear me wrong. I live in America, and I am grateful for the freedoms that we enjoy. But my ultimate allegiance will only ever be to Jesus Christ. There are layers to who we are like gender, race, political party, or citizenship. But if we are a follower of Jesus, our base identity must first be our relationship to him.

As we realize that God's Church exists across history, nations, and people groups, we recognize that holding onto one particular way of following Jesus is prideful. Right now, there are followers of Jesus living out his ways all over the world. These followers of Jesus don't look like us or sound like us. Their churches are much different than ours. But they are our brothers and sisters in Christ. Many of them live in places where it is illegal to be a follower of Jesus, yet they still do it boldly. We should pray for them regularly and learn from them as we hear their stories. Being a Christ-follower is something that transcends nationality, race, or culture. It's a delicate line to walk because we all have citizenship to an earthly nation, and that does matter. But what matters more is being citizens of God's Kingdom.

Both locally and globally, the Church preserves God's kingdom. Locally, we do this by gathering together regularly and encouraging one another. When we participate in a community like this, it keeps our lives on track. We have others to speak up when we go astray. And we have people to care for us when we are hurting. These friendships help us strive toward following Jesus. As local churches do this across the world, we form the global Church together. Even though we look and act differently, we are all part of the body of Christ. In our own cultures and communities, we actively build God's kingdom here on earth. One day his kingdom will be fully restored, but until then, it's the Church's job to preserve what Jesus left for us. We are "the salt of the earth."

DISCUSSION QUESTIONS

1. Why do you need friends who also follow Jesus?

2. What are some examples of godly friendships making a difference in your life?

3. What do your friendships look like with people who aren't Christ-followers?

4. What comes to mind when you think about the term "American Christian?" How should our citizenship in God's kingdom go beyond our other identities?

5. What does it mean to be "the salt of the earth?"

11

WHERE DO I GO FROM HERE?

In Game 6 of the 2013 NBA Finals, the Miami Heat were down 3 games to 2 to the San Antonio Spurs. With 19.4 seconds left in the game, the Heat were trailing 95-92, and all hope seemed to be lost. Their home fans were already leaving the building. Stadium personnel started to bring out ropes to block off the court for the Spurs' victory celebration. As the Heat dribbled down the court, everyone knew that the team's best player, LeBron James, would take the final shot. And with 11 seconds left, LeBron tried a 3-pointer that missed. As it bounced off the rim, another Heat player, Chris Bosh, fought for the rebound. As Bosh grabbed the rebound, his teammate, Ray Allen, was under the rim and saw an opening when his defender fell down. He immediately backpedaled to the corner of the court behind the 3-point line. Bosh passed Allen the ball right as he came into position. With 5 seconds left, Allen elevated above his defender and sank the game tying 3-pointer with a hand in his face. The Heat would later go on to win the game in overtime, and a few days later, they won Game 7 and the NBA Championship.

Take a minute and find a clip of this sequence on YouTube. Searching something like "Ray Allen Game 6 shot" should bring up several options. Ray Allen's shot was incredible. It saved the Heat's chances of winning a title that year. As you watch it, you begin to see how difficult that shot was. When Ray Allen backpedaled to the 3-point line, he did it without looking down. And somehow, his feet were exactly where they were supposed to be. In the corner of an NBA basketball court, there are 36" between the 3-point line and the out of bounds line. It's the smallest space on the court where you can take a shot. If he had a toe on the 3-point line, the shot would have only counted for 2 points, and his team would have still been behind. If his foot had been out of bounds, the shot would not have counted at all. It was so close, the officials even went to instant replay to verify what happened. But Ray Allen's feet were exactly where they were supposed to be.

Also, a defender had a hand in his face making it difficult for him to see the basket. Despite all that, he made the shot. Here's the thing about that shot, though. It wasn't luck. In interviews over the years, Ray Allen has talked about how he practiced that sequence a thousand times over his career. He would practice backpedaling to the corner over and over so he would always stay in bounds. He would practice shooting with someone putting a hand in his face so that it wouldn't bother him. Ray Allen had been *training* to take that shot for years.

Successful people aren't always lucky. Most of the time, they are prepared because of habits and training, just like Ray Allen was. The same is true for mature followers of Jesus. You may know people who are living like Jesus in a way that seems effortless. They always seem to do the right thing and have wisdom beyond understanding. Those people are not lucky. Most likely, they have spent years training to follow Jesus. Through mistakes, hardships, and the development of good habits, they know how to love their enemy, find joy in all circumstances, and stand boldly in the face of injustice.

Following Jesus is a journey, and everyone will find themselves at different places on that journey. It is not good to compare yourself to others to determine if they are further along than you. Following Jesus is not a competition. However, it can be helpful to learn from others that have traveled ahead of us. "This is what the Lord says: Stand by the roadways and look. Ask about the ancient paths, 'Which is the way to what is good?' Then take it and find rest for yourselves." (Jeremiah 6:16)

As we arrive at the end of this book, I hope you have identified two things. First, you have learned the difference between just believing that God exists and following Jesus. And second, you know where you are on your journey. As we close, I want to leave you with instructions on the way forward. It is an incredible blessing that following Jesus is a well-traveled path that many others have taken before us. We do not have to guess or hope that we are taking the right path. Following Jesus is about spending the rest of our lives training to live his way. I use the word "training" on purpose. In his book *The Life You've Always Wanted*, John Ortberg outlines the idea of trying vs. training. We do not try to follow Jesus; *we train to follow Jesus.* Trying involves sheer will power and relies on our best efforts. Training consists of developing the discipline to stick to a routine and keep going even when we fail.

Professional athletes do not "try" at their respective sports. They train to develop the necessary skills. "Don't you know that the runners in a stadium all race, but only one receives the prize? Run in such a way to win the prize. Now everyone who competes exercises self-control in everything. They do it to receive a perishable crown, but we an imperishable crown. So I do not run like one who runs aimlessly or box like one beating the air. Instead, I discipline my body and bring it under strict control, so that after preaching to others, I myself will not be disqualified." (1 Corinthians 9:24-27)

As a follower of Jesus, the way forward is training. Training means that we develop the discipline to practice the habits that are needed to make Jesus the priority in our lives. This means that we train to spend time with him each day through prayer and the study of the Bible. We train to be more like him by surrounding ourselves with others who are doing the same. We train by admitting and recognizing our mistakes to learn from them. We train by learning to fight for justice in an unjust world. We train by doing the right thing even when we don't feel like it.

How many athletes wake up early in the morning to train and think, "I really don't feel like doing this today."? All of them! No one can wake up with a perfect attitude every single day. But discipline and training allow us to continue doing what we're supposed to do even when we don't feel like it. Just like it takes athletes years of training to master a sport, it will take years of training to make following Jesus second nature to us. Don't be discouraged by that. In fact, you should be *encouraged* by that. People who are further along on the journey than you have just been through more training. You have not done anything wrong. Never feel bad about where you are on your journey. God will take you forward as you develop the habits that lead you closer to him. Over time, you will begin to see your progress and growth as the training pays off.

When you are just trying at something, failing will lead you to quit. "Oh well, at least I tried." When you are training for something, failing will motivate you to do better. "I know I can get better." This mindset is essential. After deciding to follow Jesus, you will not live a perfect life. You will sin again and make mistakes. Satan is real, and he will tempt you to do things that are not right. If you follow Jesus, you are dangerous to the enemy, and he will try to bring you down. There will be times that no matter how hard you try, you will give in to temptation. When you mess up, confess your sin to God and anyone you have hurt. Do what is necessary to make it right. Then, receive the Lord's forgiveness and move on.

This is not an excuse to do whatever you want, knowing you will be forgiven. Instead, it is meant to encourage you to work through your mistakes and shortcomings since no one is perfect. Do not let false guilt or shame beat you down over mistakes that you have made. "Therefore, there is now no condemnation for those in Christ Jesus, because the law of the Spirit of life in Christ Jesus has set you free from the law of sin and death." (Romans 8:1-2) Don't wallow in your mistakes. It will take time, and that's ok. Good things take time. The important thing is that you don't give up. Keep training yourself no matter what.

As you grow and learn in your relationship with Jesus, it is important to know that following him is costly. I do not want to sugarcoat or hide that fact from you. "Then Jesus said to his disciples, 'If anyone wants to follow after me, let him deny himself, take up his cross, and follow me. For whoever wants to save his life will lose it, but whoever loses his life because of me will find it.'" (Matthew16:24-25)

At the beginning of this book, I said that following Jesus is difficult but not complicated. The steps are clear, but to truly follow him, we have to completely deny ourselves. This is a costly and challenging step. We give up our selfish way of life and submit ourselves to live his way. Throughout church history, this has been true for every follower of Jesus. For some, it means living in the face of severe persecution for their faith and losing their own lives. For others, it means living in a way that is different from everyone else and possibly losing reputation, social status, wealth, or friendships.

As followers of Jesus living in the free world, persecution can be hard for us to fully grasp. We live in free countries where we can worship God without fear. We cannot control what context we are born into. Regardless of our situation, the most important thing for each individual is to live the life Jesus taught us, no matter what. For followers of Christ living under persecution, that means living each day knowing it might be their last. For those living in a time of prosperity, this means doing whatever it takes to find Jesus' way in our culture.

There are so many situations where it seems like we have to choose one side or the other, especially when it comes to politics or social issues. You are either on one side or another. But there is always a third way, the Jesus way. Instead of fighting for earthly organizations, we fight for his kingdom. We do not let anything else get in the way of that priority.

I am not saying that we should not be involved in political or social issues. In fact, this can be one area where we stand for justice and truth. But what I am saying is that when we engage with our culture on any of these things, we must use the lens of God's kingdom to see everything and everyone around us. As we do that, it allows us to engage our culture with humility and conviction. How do we know what Jesus' way is? As the Holy Spirit works in us through prayer, the study of the

Bible, and friendships with other believers in our lives, it becomes clearer how we should live each day. We see the world how he sees it, and we respond accordingly, even if it costs us something.

Ultimately what we're working for is the establishment of God's Kingdom. In Chapter 2, we saw how God's story ends with a "Final Resolution." This is the part of the story that hasn't happened yet. One day, Jesus will return and restore God's creation back to the way it's supposed to be. God will establish once and for all Heaven on earth. When I was a kid, the thought of Heaven was scary to me. Like many others, the first thought that came to mind was sitting on a cloud singing all day. That did not sound awesome to me. I'm not sure where that picture came from, but over the years, it has been the familiar image that many of us use for Heaven.

I have great news! Heaven will be nothing like that. To be honest, Heaven still makes me feel a little weird when I think about it. It's something that we can't know or understand, so it makes us uneasy. But what we do know for sure is that it will be better than we can ever imagine. When God restores his creation, I imagine it will be similar to what it was like at the Garden of Eden. God and human beings will live in perfect harmony while enjoying God's creation.

While Heaven on earth is a future event that we look forward to, it is still something we can experience now. As we follow Jesus, we are actively participating in building his kingdom here on earth. This world is difficult, and it's full of brokenness, pain, and sorrow.

But we live with the hope that something better is coming. It is not a wishing, uncertain hope. It is a secure, certain hope. Jesus will come back, and he will make everything right. Because of that, we live with hope, joy, and peace on earth. No matter what happens, we can face it with the knowledge that this is not the end.

      Back in Chapter 1, I talked to you about eternal life. We saw that this term isn't just referring to something in the future. Eternal life starts now. We are already participating in the life to come that Jesus promises to us. This means that God gives us the gift of confidently navigating the challenges of this life. Hopefully, after reading the rest of the book, the concept of eternal life starting now makes sense to you. As we train ourselves to follow Jesus, it becomes easier to learn the difference between joy (a virtue that never changes) and happiness (a fleeting emotion). It becomes easier to develop a "peace that surpasses all understanding" in every circumstance. It becomes easier to confidently face hopeless injustices with the security that only Jesus can give. These things don't come from believing in God and trying to be a good person. They only come from following Jesus. As a follower of Jesus, your job now is to train yourself each day to be more like him. "Let us run with endurance the race that lies before us, keeping our eyes on Jesus, the pioneer and perfecter of our faith." (Hebrews 12:1-2) It is a process that will only end after your life on earth is finished. Once your life here is done, your training is complete, and you will live in perfect harmony with the one who created you. Until then, live like someone who is training for Heaven.

"He who testifies about these things says, "Yes, I am coming soon." Amen! Come, Lord Jesus!" (Revelation 22:20)

DISCUSSION QUESTIONS

1. What are examples of skills in life that people must train for?

2. What is the difference between trying and training?

3. How do good habits help you do what is right, even when you don't feel like it?

4. Why is following Jesus costly?

5. As you finish this book, what is next?

AFTERWORD

There is so much that this book does not cover. My hope is that as you read it, it sparks the desire to learn more—and there is so much more to learn. What we have covered here is just the beginning. In Chapter 7, I talked about how spiritual habits are practices that we learn to help our faith grow. The three primary spiritual habits mentioned in this book are prayer, the study of scripture, and godly friendships. These are three great habits to start with, and you should focus on practicing them well for a while. But as you grow over time, it is so important to keep going. You will find deeper levels of knowing the heart of God. You will discover new practices that will enhance your life. This will take time, and you should not rush the process. Just know that you will find more as your relationship with Jesus grows stronger.

Throughout this book, the theme has been focusing on the step in front of us. Even though there is much to learn, you do not need to be overwhelmed by it. God will take you step by step through all of it. Psalm 119:105 says, "Your word is a lamp for my feet and a light on my path." If you think about holding a light on a dark path, you can only see what is right in front of you. You cannot see the end. You can't even see past a few steps. Your journey in your relationship with God is the same. Your responsibility is always the step right in front of you. Don't worry that you cannot see the rest of the path. It's not your job to know the whole path. It's your job to take each step.

As you do that, God will bring you closer and closer to himself. You will learn and grow in so many different ways. You will continue to learn more about him through the study of Scripture, regular prayer, a community of believers, and books like this one. Be a life-long learner. Never think you have it all figured out. Continue to do things that help you grow, and I promise that you will never run out of things to learn.

As you finish this book, I want you to take a minute and think about what is next for you. Which one of the steps in this book do you need to focus on? What are some things down the road that you will need in your life? As you feel ready for each one, you can confidently take that step. There is so much to learn about our faith, and things that seem impossible to learn now will become possible for you to learn over time. You may not be a reader, and that's ok. Find whatever method works for you, but never stop learning. There are many ways to do this, and we all experience them differently. The important thing is that we're moving forward. Follow the journey and take the steps. As followers of Jesus, the journey might be different, but we're all headed to the same place. See you there.

ENDNOTES

1. J. Scott Duvall and J. Daniel Hays, *Grasping God's Word, 2nd Ed.: A Hand's-On Approach to Reading, Interpreting, and Applying the Bible.* (Grand Rapids, MI: Zondervan, 2005), 412-413.
2. *Ibid.*
3. Craig Blomberg, *The New American Commentary: Vol. 22, Matthew.* (Nashville, TN: B&H Publishing, 1992), 434.

Connect with the Authors

Email: square1book@gmail.com

Instagram: @zach_wright_ @duvall

Facebook: facebook.com/Wright.Zachary

Printed in Great Britain
by Amazon